The 500 Hidden Secrets of
NEW YORK

INTRODUCTION

You've picked up this book, so naturally we assume you've got an inquisitive mind and you don't want to settle for the ordinary. That's why we created this guide, for people like you – the ones who dig deeper, who long to find a true connection to a city's *zeitgeist*.

The suggestions in this book come from a pair of writers who live and thrive on the NYC lifestyle, and can help you weed through an often overwhelming amount of choices. Starting with dining, our streamlined picks are all winners and cover the gamut, from cheap eats to orchestrated tastings. Listed also are off-the-beaten-path museums, memorials, and historic parts of the city that are truly enlightening. When you're ready to stop for a cocktail, coffee, or glass of wine somewhere, we've got you covered with tried-and-true destinations. You'll find out how to enjoy nature within the city – on the water and in the parks – or on a mini-escape. Also included are hot shopping spots, ideas for entertaining nights out, and a handful of hotels that can enhance a stay.

NYC is constantly evolving, and our selections indicate a definite shift to creative happenings in Brooklyn, especially for millennials. Queens also factors into this shift, as the island of Manhattan becomes more exclusive and pricey. The focus in Manhattan is decidedly downtown for the best in nightlife, dining, and shopping. Midtown continues to be for daytime forays, museums, and theater at night.

We hope that our flurry of insider suggestions will help make your experience more personal and memorable, and will inspire you to make your own discoveries.

HOW TO USE THIS BOOK?

This guide lists 500 things you need to know about New York in 100 different categories. Most of these are places to visit, with practical information like the address and sometimes info on making reservations. Others are bits of information that help you get to know the city and its people. The purpose of this guide is to inspire you to explore the city, but it doesn't cover every aspect from A to Z.

The places in this guide are given an address, including the neighborhood (for example 'Lower East Side' or 'Greenwich Village'), and a number. The neighborhood and number allow you to find the places on the maps at the beginning of the book: first look for the map of the corresponding neighborhood, then look for the right number. A word of caution however: these maps are not detailed enough to allow you to find specific locations in the city. They are included to give you a sense of where places are, and whether they are close by other places of interest. You can obtain an excellent map from any tourist office or in most hotels. Or the addresses can be located on a smartphone.

Please also bear in mind that cities change all the time. The chef who hits a high note one day may be uninspiring on the day you happen to visit. The bar considered one of the 5 most funky bars on the Lower East Side might be empty on the night you're there. This is obviously a highly personal selection. You might not always agree with it. If you want to leave a comment, recommend a bar or reveal your favorite secret place, please visit the website *www.the500hiddensecrets.com* – you'll also find free tips and the latest news about the series there – or follow *@500hiddensecrets* on Instagram and leave a comment.

THE AUTHORS

Michiel Vos is a Dutch-American correspondent for Dutch and Belgian TV and radio, as well as a commentator on European American politics for *Charlie Rose*. In his personal documentary series *My America*, which aired both in Belgium and The Netherlands, he documented his experiences in America as a European immigrant. Michiel regularly gives his opinion on US politics and its pop culture on the Dutch daily late night talk show *RTL Late Night*, on *EenVandaag*, and on several Belgian talk shows. He is a sought-after speaker for European companies, entrepreneurs and interested groups, wanting to know more about his adopted homeland, America.

Michiel lives in Manhattan with his wife, filmmaker Alexandra Pelosi and their two boys. Follow him on Twitter @americanvos.

Lifelong New York resident **Ellen Swandiak** first became enamored with NYC while attending Parsons School of Design, which inspired a move to a ground-floor apartment in the far West Village. Living in the most colorful and bohemian part of the city taught her to navigate the winding streets of downtown and get to know its many wonderful shops and eateries. In 2005 Ellen moved to a Gramercy high-rise with a winning view of the Empire State Building. Here the idea of a blog was born, now known as *Hobnob Magazine* (hobnobmag.com) which reports on all her loves: food, drink, style, fun – and parties. As a creative party thrower, Ellen uses ideas inspired by the best chefs and mixologists to include in her fun party themes designed to help people entertain. She can often be spotted, camera in hand, at stylish restaurants and bars, tasting events, and art openings, with her designer eye on the lookout for all that is clever.

Not a day goes by without someone asking Ellen for a tip, but she claims she could not have come up with all these super suggestions without the help of a few friends, so she wishes to thank in particular: Paulina Kajankova who helped name many a fashionable shop, Ronit Schlam, whose knowledge of dance and theater came in handy, and Tom Grant, for letting her run suggestions by him, and who had some great ones of his own.

NEW YORK

overview

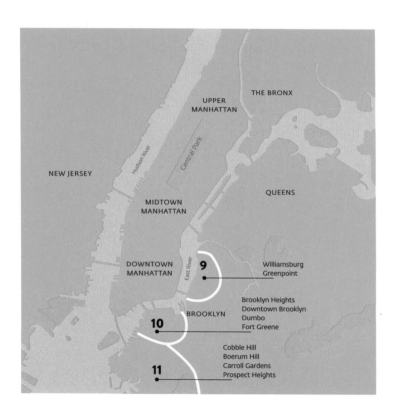

THE BRONX

UPPER
MANHATTAN

NEW JERSEY

Hudson River

Central Park

MIDTOWN
MANHATTAN

QUEENS

DOWNTOWN
MANHATTAN

East River

9

Williamsburg
Greenpoint

BROOKLYN

Brooklyn Heights
Downtown Brooklyn
Dumbo
Fort Greene

10

Cobble Hill
Boerum Hill
Carroll Gardens
Prospect Heights

11

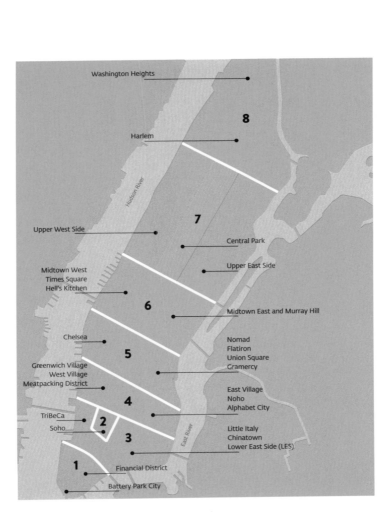

Washington Heights

8

Harlem

Hudson River

7

Upper West Side

Central Park

Upper East Side

Midtown West
Times Square
Hell's Kitchen

6

Midtown East and Murray Hill

Chelsea

5

Nomad
Flatiron
Union Square
Gramercy

Greenwich Village
West Village
Meatpacking District

4

East Village
Noho
Alphabet City

TriBeCa

2

Soho

3

Little Italy
Chinatown
Lower East Side (LES)

East River

1

Financial District

Battery Park City

Map 1

DOWNTOWN MANHATTAN

FINANCIAL DISTRICT
and BATTERY PARK CITY

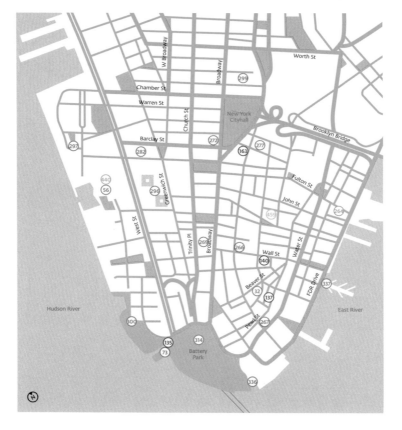

Map 2

DOWNTOWN MANHATTAN

SOHO

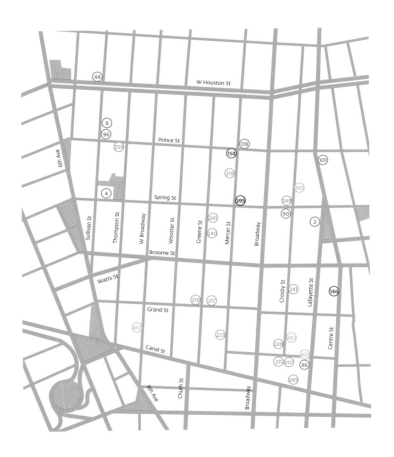

Map 3

DOWNTOWN MANHATTAN

TRIBECA, SOHO *and* LITTLE ITALY

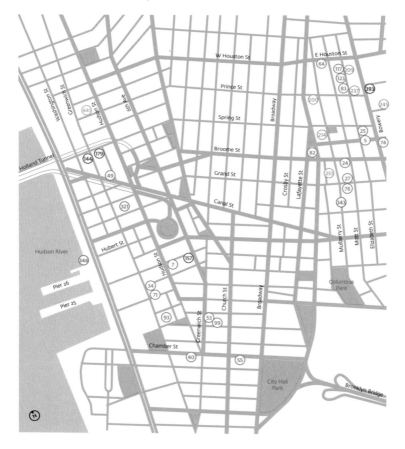

CHINATOWN *and* LOWER EAST SIDE

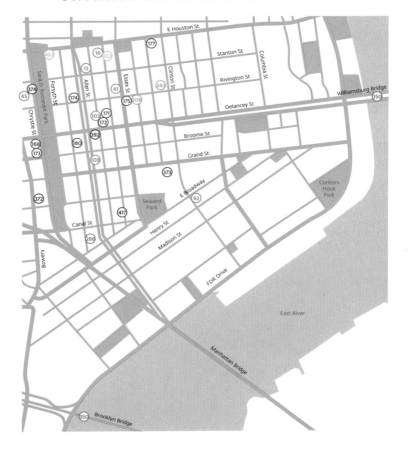

Map 4

DOWNTOWN MANHATTAN
GREENWICH VILLAGE, WEST VILLAGE
and MEATPACKING DISTRICT

EAST VILLAGE, NOHO
and ALPHABET CITY

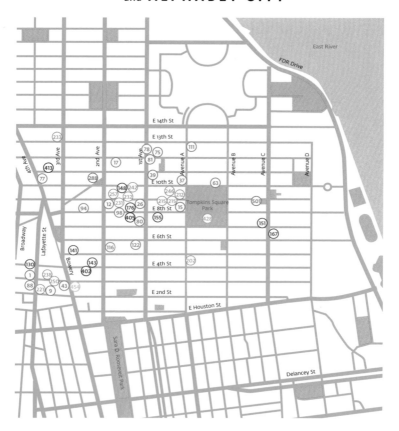

Map 5

MIDTOWN MANHATTAN

CHELSEA

NOMAD, FLATIRON, UNION SQUARE *and* GRAMERCY

W 29th St — E 29th St
72

452

W 27th St — E 27th St

Madison Ave

Park Ave S

Lexington Ave

3rd Ave

5th Ave

109

196

W 25th St — E 25th St
10

11
080

Madison
Square
Park

46

W 23rd St — E 23rd St

Flatiron
Building

W 22nd St — E 22nd St
185
273

236
410

112

Gramercy
Park

W 20th St — E 20th St
303

259

131

225
246 109

Irving Pl

3rd Ave

126 156

W 18th St — E 18th St
239

235
355

293

3
292

W 16th St — E 16th St

Union
Square
Park

W 14th St — E 14th St

Broadway

5th Ave

Map 6

MIDTOWN MANHATTAN

MIDTOWN WEST,
TIMES SQUARE *and* HELL'S KITCHEN

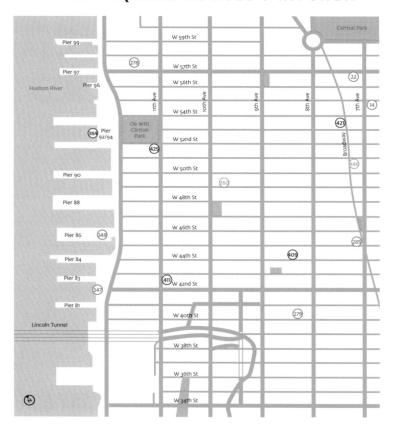

Central Park

Pier 99

W 59th St

278 W 57th St

Pier 97 W 56th St

22

Pier 96

Hudson River W 54th St 14

11th Ave 10th Ave 9th Ave 8th Ave 7th Ave

384 Pier 92/94 421

De Witt Clinton Park W 52nd St

425 Broadway

W 50th St 449

Pier 90 260 W 48th St

Pier 88 W 46th St

Pier 86 348 W 44th St 409 285

Pier 84 W 42nd St 411

Pier 83 411

347 Pier 81 W 40th St 279

Lincoln Tunnel W 38th St

W 36th St

N W 34th St

MIDTOWN EAST *and* MURRAY HILL

Central Park

(339)

(401)

E 59th St

(276)

(280)

W 57th St

E 57th St

E 56th St

(378)

E 56th St

6th Ave

5th Ave

3rd Ave

2nd Ave

1st Ave

(51)

(161)

E 54th St

(201) MoMA (125)

(139)

(165)

(54)

E 52nd St

(170)

E 50th St

Madison Ave

Park Ave

Lexington Ave

E 50th St

(422)(423)(424)(437)(274)

(376)

E 48th St

E 46th St

E 46th St

E 44th St

(136)(270)

(310)

(60)

E 44th St

1st Ave Tunnel

East River

(182)

Grand
Central
Terminal

(128)

(124) W 42nd St

(438)

(121)

(59)

(271)

Bryant Park (100)

(181)
E 40th St

(416)

(468)

Broadway

(458)

E 38th St

3rd Ave

2nd Ave

FDR Drive

Madison Ave

Park Ave

Lexington Ave

(305)

E 36th St

(31)

E 34th St

(281)

(256)↓(290)

(224)↓

(100)

(19)↓

Map 7

UPPER WEST SIDE, CENTRAL PARK

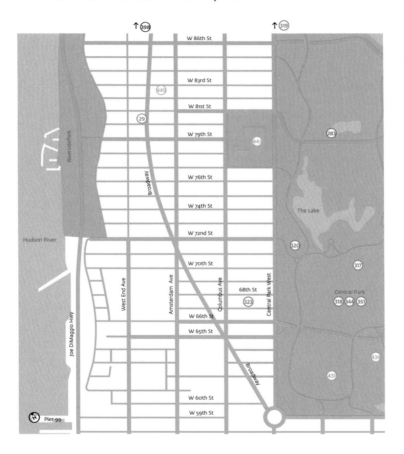

UPPER EAST SIDE

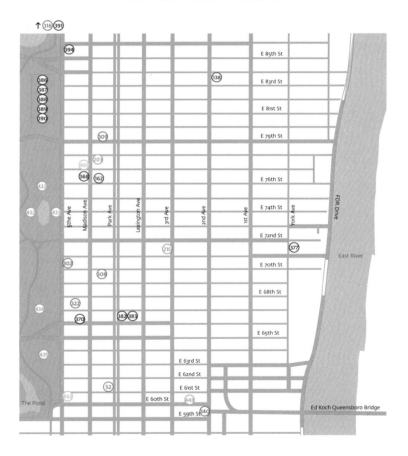

Map 8

UPPER MANHATTAN

HARLEM *and* WASHINGTON HEIGHTS

313 304 ↑

THE BRONX

301

331

W 155th St

Hudson River

Harlem River Dr

Harlem

W 145th St

Frederick Douglass Blvd

Adam Clayton Powell Jr Blvd

Malcolm X Blvd / Lenox Ave

W 135th St

Broadway

Amsterdam Ave

371

5th Ave

Madison Ave

Park Ave

Dr Martin Luther King Jr Blvd

298

287

295

Lexington Ave

3rd Ave

2nd Ave

1st Ave

Riverside Park

116th St

289

110th St

Central Park N

Central Park

Ⓝ

Map 9

BROOKLYN

WILLIAMSBURG *and* GREENPOINT

Map 10

BROOKLYN

BROOKLYN HEIGHTS, DOWNTOWN, DUMBO *and* FORT GREENE

Map 11

BROOKLYN

COBBLE HILL, BOERUM HILL, CARROLL GARDENS *and* PROSPECT HEIGHTS

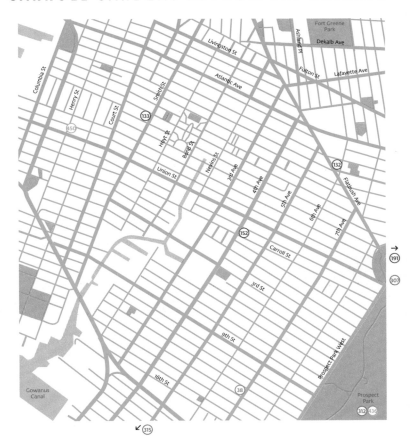

THE BUTCHER'S DAUGHTER

125 PLACES TO EAT OR BUY GOOD FOOD

———

5 places for
BREAKFAST & BREAD

---

1   **LAFAYETTE GRAND CAFÉ & BAKERY**

380 Lafayette St
(at Great Jones)
East Village ④
+1 212 533 3000
www.lafayetteny.com

Is it the leather booths, enticing case of pastries, or the Belle Époque atmosphere? Never mind why, we love this place. Relax and enjoy artisanal breads, muffins, and assorted pastries baked right on the premises. Or, start your day with one of their fresh-pressed juices to accompany a lively selection of fruit, cereals, eggs, and pancakes.

2   **JACK'S WIFE FREDA**

224 Lafayette St
(betw Spring and
Kenmare St)
Soho ②
+1 212 510 8550
jackswifefreda.com

An eatery with the sweet ambiance of home. Owned by a husband and wife team – who named the place after their grandparents, who also inspired the menu. Great egg dishes with some Mediterranean flavors thrown in. Rosewater waffles come topped with Lebanese yogurt, mixed berries and honey syrup. Note the cute messages on their sugar packets.

3 BREADS BAKERY

18 East 16th St
(betw Union Square W
and 5th Ave)
Union Square ⑤
+1 212 633 2253
www.breadsbakery.com

Here breads come in all shapes and varieties. Challah takes center stage, covered with all sorts of nuts and seeds, among adorable little whole-grain rolls and dense pumpernickel. Pastries, like chocolate rugelach and cookies compete for your attention. Scout out their kiosks on the corner of Bryant park (42nd and 6th Ave) and at Lincoln Center (1890 Broadway).

4 DOMINIQUE ANSEL BAKERY

189 Spring St
(betw Sullivan and
Thompson St)
Soho ②
+1 212 219 2773
www.dominiqueansel.com

Before opening this bakery, Ansel was exec pastry chef at 3-Michelin-star Daniel, and has moved on to invent a croissant-doughnut hybrid dubbed 'the cronut' whose popularity causes lines around the block. See why everyone loves the fried dough rolled in sugar, stuffed with cream and topped with glaze. Line starts before 8 am.

5 THE BUTCHER'S DAUGHTER

19 Kenmare St
(betw Elizabeth St
and Bowery)
Nolita ③
+1 212 219 3434
www.thebutchers
daughter.com

Ironically named, this spot is a wonderland for vegans and vegetarians. Pop in to get your juice fix, or coconut yogurt parfait, made with ingredients from local farms. They also offer a bunch of egg dishes, plus avocado on toast. There's a second outlet in West Village, on 581 Hudson Street at Bank Street.

5 *friendly places for*
B R U N C H

---

6 ROSEMARY'S
18 Greenwich Avenue
(at W 10th St)
Greenwich Village ④
+1 212 647 1818
www.rosemarysnyc.com

The rooftop garden put this place on the map but it's the menu and the ambiance that kept it on the map. There's a long wait sometimes, but enjoying your Italian dish straight from the produce grown on the roof is worth it. In summer French doors open onto the street.

7 BUBBY'S
120 Hudson St
(at N Moore St)
TriBeCa ③
+1 212 219 0666
www.bubbys.com

If you're in for a true American brunch, go to Bubby's. These guys make a point of serving upscale, classic American dishes in a rustic, laid back setting. Try one of their biscuits – a Southern specialty – topped with sausage, jalapeño and eggs, or fried chicken. There's a second outlet close to the Highline.

8 ONCE UPON A TART
135 Sullivan St (betw
Prince and Houston St)
Soho ②
+1 212 387 8869
www.onceuponatart.com

Parts of Soho are bustling, commercial, and dominated by multinational chains. Luckily, the west side still retains its original quirkier and quieter vibe. That's where you'll find Tart, complete with Parisian park-style chairs outside. Try the Alsatian apple tart.

9   **THE SMILE**

26 Bond St (betw
Lafayette and Bowery)
Noho ④
+1 646 329 5836
www.thesmilenyc.com

This mix of a general store and cafe exudes a rustic, upstate vibe and is a hangout for the young, stylish, arty crowd. Head underground to enjoy the Belgian waffles with caramelized figs. And whatever you order, make sure to get a side of crispy sweet potato hash browns. Fresh muffins, scones, and bread too.

10   **UPLAND**

345 Park Avenue South
(at 26th St)
Nomad ⑤
+1 212 686 1006
www.uplandnyc.com

California cuisine is served in a high-ceiling industrial space, with room to breathe. Try the fresh little gem salad, which is so large it's a must share. In the egg category, the Spanish frittata with roasted garlic mayonnaise, and espelette is something unique. Creative pizzas and fabulous bottles of wine under 50 dollars.

8 ONCE UPON A TART

5 interesting places to
DO LUNCH

---

11 LA PECORA BIANCA
1133 Broadway
(at 26th St)
Nomad ⑤
+1 212 498 9696
www.lapecorabianca.com

La Pecora Bianca is a perfect place to do lunch and sample nicely-priced Italian specialties in an airy, industrial whitewashed space. Seasonal and local influence the menu, and even factor into the homemade pastas using whole-wheat and gluten-free grains. The coffee bar transforms into a wine bar later in the day.

12 VESELKA
144 Second Avenue
(betw St Marks Place
and E 9th St)
East Village ④
+1 212 228 9682
www.veselka.com

This place is a leftover from when the neighborhood was mostly East European. The menu features *borscht*, beef stroganoff, stuffed cabbage, and a mean Ukrainian keilbasa (smoked pork sausage). Open 24 hours, so also the perfect destination after an East Village pub crawl.

13 THE MEATBALL SHOP
84 Stanton St (betw
Allen and Orchard St)
Lower East Side ③
+1 212 982 8895
www.themeatballshop.com

These guys have turned the humble meatball into a superstar. Choose a meat – spicy pork, traditional beef, chicken, or veggie – add a sauce and some sides or get yours on a 'hero' (meaning a big sandwich). A bit packed inside but delicious and no fuss. Kid friendly.

14 RADIANCE TEA HOUSE & BOOKS

158 West 55th St
(betw 6th and 7th Ave)
Midtown West ⑥
+1 212 217 0442
www.radiancetea.com

A Chinese teahouse with dim-sum-style small plates on the menu. Tucked inside a bookstore, you'll find a peaceful ambiance and an extensive selection of exotic blends of hot and iced teas. For lunch they offer a series of 'box' lunches, 4 items served in a tray with compartments. Peruse the shop for traditional teapots, teacups and teas.

15 CRIF DOGS

113 St Marks Place
(betw Ave A and 1st Ave)
East Village ④
+1 212 614 2728
www.crifdogs.com

A deep-fried menu of creative hot dogs is the gig here. Dogs come every which way – even a veggie version, and classic NY, which just gets some sauerkraut. Choose from 28 toppings to create your own signature dog, or go for one of their tried-and-true combos like Chihuahua: wrapped in bacon, topped with avodado, sour cream and salsa.

11 LA PECORA BIANCA

5 *places where*
TIME STANDS STILL

16 **KATZ'S DELICATESSEN**
205 East Houston St
(at Ludlow St)
Lower East Side ③
+1 212 254 2246
www.katzsdelicatessen.com

New York without Katz's would not
be New York. Stick to the classics: the
overstuffed corned beef or pastrami sandwiches on rye. While you're there, check
out the original World War II sign: 'Send
a salami to your boy in the army' and that
iconic table where Harry met Sally.

17 **JOHN'S OF 12TH STREET**
302 East 12th St
(betw 1st and 2nd Ave)
East Village ④
+1 212 475 9531
*www.johns
of12thstreet.com*

No-frills East Village classic. The place
advertises itself as old-school and rightly
so. The red sauce that comes with the pasta
is the real deal, reminding you either of
grandma or of a summer in Italy long ago.
Try the chicken Parmigiana. Update: vegan
dishes also grace the menu. Cash only.

18 **ZUM STAMMTISCH**
69-46 Myrtle Avenue
(at 70th St)
Glendale, Queens
+1 718 386 3014
www.zumstammtisch.com

This is of course a German restaurant,
where main courses are massive, pork
Schnitzel, *Sauerbraten*, and all kinds of
Wurst. The Tyrolean-style place was founded in 1972 by German immigrant John
Lehner and is now run by his sons Hans
und Werner. *Zum Stammtisch* translates
to 'at the table for regulars'.

16 KATZ'S DELICATESSEN

19 **MARCHI'S RESTAURANT**

251 East 31st St
(at 2nd Ave)
Midtown ⑥
+1 212 679 2494
*www.marchi
restaurant.com*

Signor and Signora Marchi opened it in 1930, now their sons run the place. No sign on the outside of the brownstone, with its beautiful garden area, and no menu inside. People have been eating the same 5-course dinner here for 85 years – antipasti, lasagna, crisp fried fish, roast chicken and fruit dessert.

20 **SPAIN**

113 West 13th St
(betw 6th and 7th Ave)
Greenwich Village ④
+1 212 203 5719
*www.spain
restaurantny.com*

Occupied by neighborhood regulars and youngsters that have found the place word-of-mouth. The 81-year old owner is also the bartender who will greet you wearing a bright red tuxedo jacket. Great spot for lingering. Tapas are served at the bar with classic 1960s cocktails like the Side Car, Rob Roy, and Grasshopper.

22 BROOKLYN DINER

5
CHARMING
restaurants with character

---

21 **CHUMLEY'S**
86 Bedford St (betw
Grove and Barrow St)
Greenwich Village ④
+1 212 675 2081
*www.chumleys
newyork.com*

A true speakeasy which existed in its location from 1922 to 2007, always behind a nondescript door on a quiet part of Bedford Street. Today the space has been refurbished to honor and celebrate its famous literary past with book covers and portraits of all the writers who once frequented the place. A gem.

22 **BROOKLYN DINER**
212 West 57th St (betw
7th Ave and Broadway)
Midtown East ⑥
+1 212 977 1957
www.brooklyndiner.com

This nostalgic diner is around the corner from Carnegie Hall and close to Central Park. It's outfitted in plush brown leather stools and banquettes, and booths adorned with brass nameplates of celebrity patrons. Go for the cheeseburger with fried battered onions on top, or their popular chicken potpie, or a milkshake.

23 THE BEATRICE INN

285 West 12th St (betw
W 4th St and 8th Ave)
West Village ④
+1 212 675 2808
www.thebeatriceinn.com

Downstairs, on a cute block in the West Village, this clubby, upscale spot boasts lovely touches and grand architectural details. Tiled fireplaces, bronze mirrors, and paintings of animals create the feeling of home, albeit a rich person's home. Exposed brick and the low-ceiling bar create an intimate, friendly atmosphere with food that's creatively American.

24 OFICINA 1M

371 Broome St
(at Mott St)
Nolita ③
+1 718 431 3332
www.oficina.nyc

In honor of Italy's Mille Miglia race route, this adorable space is filled with car memorabilia. The front is a cafe for those looking for take out, but do stay to experience breakfast, lunch, or dinner. Recommended: the lightest chickpea gnocchi bathed in gorgonzola fondue, bacon, and roman cabbage. Bread is baked fresh here daily.

25 PIETRO NOLITA

174 Elizabeth St (betw
Kenmare and Spring St)
Nolita ③
+1 646 998 4999
www.pietronolita.com

People are abuzz about this newcomer whose decor is done with one color only: pink. A heavenly spot for Instagrammers. The owners come from the world of fashion, so have created a menu of healthy Italian delights for those watching their figures. Your souvenir: a signature t-shirt that says 'Pink As Fuck'. Open for breakfast, lunch, and dinner.

5 specialized
FOOD SHOPS

---

26 **EAST VILLAGE MEAT MARKET / J. BACZYNSKY**
139 2nd Avenue
(betw 8th and 9th St)
East Village ④
+1 212 228 5590
*www.eastvillage
meatmarket.com*

One of the city's favorite butcher shops with an enduring history, this market is a treasure in what is known as Little Ukraine. Expect high quality and reasonable prices. Go back in time with their old-fashioned *kielbasa* creations and attentive service. If you find yourself in New York during October, join them in celebrating Pierogi day.

27 **DI PALO'S FINE FOODS**
200 Grand St
(betw Mott and
Mulberry St)
Little Italy ③
+1 212 226 1033

A 100-year-old market with outrageously good Italian specialities. So good, there is usually a line that wraps around the corner. It's take-out only, so get some goodies to-go and have yourself a picnic. Tasting helps you decide. Go for the fresh mozzarella and the fresh porchetta.

28 **DÉPANNEUR**
242 Wythe Avenue
(at N 3rd St)
Williamsburg ⑨
+1 347 227 8424
www.depanneur.com

Here's a great stop in Williamsburg: a market, deli, and coffee shop in one. The grocery items are upscale – how could it be otherwise with such a delicious name. Sandwiches here are creative – like the proscuitto, fig jam and fresh mozzarella.

29   ZABAR'S

2245 Broadway
(at W 80th St)
Upper West Side ⑦
+1 212 787 2000
www.zabars.com

The Sunday morning ritual for many upper west siders. This 'temple of fish' was founded by Louis and Lilian Zabar in 1934 and is still going strong three generations later. Be seduced by all kinds and often hard to find smoked fish, caviar, dried fruit, cheeses, meats, and olives, all of the best quality.

30   MURRAY'S CHEESE

254 Bleecker St
(betw 6th and 7th St)
Greenwich Village ④
+1 212 243 3289
www.murrayscheese.com

A NYC legend on Bleecker Street has expanded into a mega foodie playground. In addition to offering a mind-boggling selection of cheeses, they've got a market loaded with packaged goods, a bulging charcuterie section, and a take-out area featuring decadent grilled cheese sandwiches. There's space upstairs for eating or attending a class.

29 ZABAR'S

5
STEAKHOUSES
not Peter Luger's

---

31   **KEENS STEAKHOUSE**
72 West 36th St
(at 6th Ave)
Midtown ⑥
+1 212 947 3636
www.keens.com

Opened in 1885, this steakhouse takes you back in time with its patrons' 90.000 clay pipes, numbered and mounted on the ceiling. The mutton chop is popular, but all the cuts of meat are extraordinary. Be prepared for enormous portions. A clubby, Victorian vibe in the bar accompanies its extensive single malt selection.

32   **DELMONICO'S**
56 Beaver St
(at South William St)
Financial District ①
+1 212 509 1144
www.delmonicos
restaurant.com

Fancy? Yes, luxurious even. Housed in a stunning triangular building way downtown, the Delmonico brothers opened this place in 1837. Known for the large wine cellar and as the birthplace of the Delmonico steak, a juicy cut of rib eye served with a single onion ring on top.

33   **OLD HOMESTEAD**
56 Ninth Avenue
(betw 14th and 15th St)
Meatpacking District ④
+1 212 242 9040
www.theoldhomestead
steakhouse.com

Located on the edge of the Meatpacking District, this place existed when the area actually was a center of meat distribution for the city, in 1868. Marked by the iconic lifesize cow that sits atop the entrance. Be prepared to spend – on colossal crab cakes, and signature prime rib – as you dine with fellow VIPs.

34 AMERICAN CUT

363 Greenwich St
(betw Franklin and
Harrison St)
TriBeCa ③
+1 212 226 4736
www.americancut
steakhouse.com

For something a little more of this century, check out Chef Marc Forgione's take on the steakhouse. He pioneered a pastrami spice rub to flavor his rib eye. Top your steak with one of five sauces or farm fresh egg or bone marrow. Raw bar includes his signature chili lobster. Two locations in Manhattan.

35 STRIP HOUSE

13 East 12th St
(betw University Pl
and 5th Ave)
Greenwich Village ④
+1 212 328 0000
www.striphouse.com

Alluding to the name, red leather banquettes, photos of pin ups and dim lighting set the scene in this underground lair. In addition to classic steaks like the New York Strip, they offer a full raw bar, and the usual sides with a little more: goose-fat potatoes and black truffle creamed spinach, are taste sensations.

32 DELMONICO'S

5 authentic places for
BAGELS

---

36 MURRAY'S BAGELS

500 Sixth Avenue
(betw 12th and 13th St)
Greenwich Village ④
+1 212 462 2830
www.murraysbagels.com

Nothing is more New York than bagels, and this one is our favorite. Until recently Murray's refused to toast their bagels, so convinced they were about their outstanding fare. Get the egg sandwich or any bagel with lox and cream cheese and enjoy on the bench outside.

37 TOMPKINS SQUARE BAGELS

165 Avenue A
(at E 10th St)
East Village ④
+1 646 351 6520
www.tompkinssquare
bagels.com

Bagels done the traditional way: rolled by hand, then boiled before baking. Twenty seven cream cheese flavors accompany the bagels, including the surprising, pastel-colored Birthday Cake, delightful for kids. As for bagel varieties, they also carry five types of gluten-free bagels and a spelt bagel. Long lines on weekends. So popular, they opened two more locations.

38 BAGEL HOLE

400 Seventh Avenue
(betw 12th and 13th St)
Park Slope, Brooklyn ⑪
+1 718 788 4014
www.bagelhole.net

Mayor Bill de Blasio, calls it 'The bagel you would have gotten a century ago'. Their winning formula uses malt instead of sugar, and can be enjoyed with or without cream cheese (or 'schmear' in proper New York lingo).

39 BLACK SEED

176 First Avenue
(at E 11th St)
East Village ④
+1 646 484 5718
www.blackseedbagels.com

Montreal's interpretation of the bagel. Slightly smaller, these are hand rolled, boiled in honey water, then baked in a wood-fired oven. Old-style mosaic tiles and taupe geometric wood benches make up the scene. Creative sandwiches in addition to the usual bagel mix. Try the pretty pink Tobiko cream cheese with smoked salmon. Other locations in Nolita and Battery Park.

40 ZUCKER'S BAGELS & SMOKED FISH

146 Chambers St
(betw West Broadway
and Greenwich St)
TriBeCa ③
+1 212 608 5844
www.zuckersbagels.com

Owner Matt Pomerantz grew up eating in all the Jewish restaurants that once graced the neighborhood, and left his job on Wall Street to run Zucker's. They keep it real in an ever more gentrifying TriBeCa with 13 types of smoked and pickled fish, 9 cream cheeses, and 16 styles of bagels.

36 MURRAY'S BAGELS

The 5 best
HIPSTER
hangouts

---

41 SONS OF ESSEX

133 Essex St
(betw Rivington and
Stanton St)
Lower East Side ③
+1 212 674 7100
www.sonsofessexnyc.com

Basically a night club with food, or a clubby restaurant if you will, where folks arrive dressed up and ready to party. Though quite good, the food is not the object here, the party atmosphere is. Go behind the deli storefront to enter a bustling bar scene in an eclectic setting with DJ and occasional celebrity drop-ins.

42 DINER

85 Broadway
(at Berry St)
Williamsburg ⑨
+1 718 486 3077
www.dinernyc.com

Cool is key here even though it has been around for a while, the neighborhood (southern stretch of Williamsburg) has changed and it has been noted that more visitors – foreign and not – frequent this place than before. Set in a narrow metal dining car from the twenties. Creative, hand-done menus.

43 THE WREN

344 Bowery
(betw Bond and 3rd St)
East Village ④
+1 212 388 0148
www.thewrennyc.com

Six blocks from Washington Square Park and close to the Bowery Hotel, this East Village hang out on the Bowery feels like a studied English farmhouse, but with a hipster ambiance. Of course, you can order your fish and chips and fried calamari, but since they are known more for their cocktails, focus on these.

44 MISS LILY'S

132 West Houston St
(at Sullivan St)
Soho ②
+1 646 588 5375
www.misslilys.com

A cool Caribbean hangout that has its own radio station on the premises, so you can get your reggae fix while chowing down. Snack on the jerk corn topped with mayo and toasted coconut, hot pepper shrimp, or grilled branzino in scotch bonnet brown butter. Photos of Grace Jones grace the walls for your viewing pleasure.

45 FREEMANS

End of Freemans Alley
(off Rivington St betw
Chrystie St and Bowery)
Lower East Side ③
+1 212 420 0012
www.freemans
restaurant.com

Hidden in an alley off Rivington Street a dual level of small rooms create the feel of a clandestine colonial American tavern exemplified by its rugged decor, creaky wooden floors, and a glut of taxidermy. The menu is all American as well. Try the whole grilled trout, served with thyme, garlic oil and lemon.

44 MISS LILY'S

45 FREEMANS

5 must try
BURGERS

---

46   SHAKE SHACK
Madison Square Park
(SE corner off 23rd St)
Flatiron ⑤
+1 212 889 6600
www.shakeshack.com

The original mothership of Danny
Meyer's global chain has served its much
desired burger – an upscale rendition of
its fast-food cousins – here since 2004.
Stand in line and order all the toppings.
Or download the official Shake Shack app
to order ahead and choose a pick-up time.

47   THE SPANIARD
190 West 4th St
(at Barrow St)
Greenwich Village ④
+1 212 918 1986
www.thespaniardnyc.com

Great spot to meet attractive people, slink
into a leather banquette, and indulge
in upscale pub food. They're known for
their extensive whiskey selection and
the Smash Burger, which consists of a
double order of smashed patties, cooked
crispy and topped with American cheese,
lettuce, and pickles.

48   BAR SARDINE
183 West 10th St
(at W 4th St)
West Village ④
+1 646 360 3705
www.barsardinenyc.com

A cozy village spot that serves food till the
wee hours. Its renowned Fedora Burger
is named after its sister restaurant a few
doors down, and comes topped with
crunchy shoestring potatoes, pickles,
onions, smoked cheddar and BBQ mayo.
A no reservation policy will have you
waiting, but it's worth it.

49 HAROLD'S MEAT + THREE

2 Renwick St (betw
Canal and Spring St)
TriBeCa ③
+1 212 390 8484
www.haroldsmeat
andthree.com

Styled after cafeterias in the South, this place offers a meat selection with, yes, a selection of three sides. There is an all-you-can-eat salad bar too. A great spot if you are with a group that has different food preferences. Their burger is of the double-patty variety, an upscale version of the fast-food variety.

50 VIA CAROTA

51 Grove St (betw
Bleecker and W 4th St)
West Village ④
+1 212 255 1962
www.viacarota.com

This seasonally-driven Italian restaurant offers a most unusual burger, known as the hand-chopped grass-fed steak. Served sans bun, it is charred on two sides and red in the middle. Strictly for meat loving purists. They've filled the space with antique china and other charming touches, from the team of chefs that own Buvette and I Sodi.

46 SHAKE SHACK

5 of the best
MEDIA HANGOUTS

---

51 **MICHAEL'S NEW YORK**
24 West 55th St
(betw 5th and 6th Ave)
Midtown ⑥
+1 212 767 0555
*www.michaels
newyork.com*

No one comes to Michael's to hide. See and be seen is the game. Although power lunches seem to have been replaced by crumbs in your keyboard as leftovers of your lonely lunch, New York City's economy still largely runs on 2 businesses: finance and media. The latter's dealmakers do lunch here.

52 **THE REGENCY BAR AND GRILL**
AT: LOEWS REGENCY HOTEL
NEW YORK
540 Park Avenue
(at E 61st St)
Upper East Side ⑦
+1 212 759 4100
www.loewshotels.com

Brokers came together here during New York's near financial collapse in the 1970s to right the ship: they did, and the power breakfast was born. Instead of going hipster downtown, power up at this newly renovated institution and enjoy its cushy opulence. You may just spot some politicians and other players doing their thing.

53 **THE ODEON**

145 West Broadway
(at Thomas St)
TriBeCa ③
+1 212 233 0507
*www.theodeon
restaurant.com*

Since the editors at Condé Nast publishing have descended on 1 World Trade Center, grand ol' Odeon has been the place of choice to frequent. Once the hub of 1980's nightlife and the famous hangout of TV's *Saturday Night Live* cast. Gorgeous space. The mini doughnuts with jellies for dessert are it.

54 **'21' CLUB**

21 West 52nd St
(betw 5th and 6th Ave)
Midtown ⑥
+1 212 582 7200
www.21club.com

You basically get a hint for what the '21' Club is when you watch the scene in Oliver Stone's *Wall Street*, where swashbuckler Michael 'Gordon Gekko' Douglas tells Charlie Sheen to buy a better suit. Dark, formal, with a grown-up vibe, and so much NY history. This is where New York rainmakers converge.

55 **RACINES NY**

94 Chambers St (betw
Broadway and Church St)
TriBeCa ③
+1 212 227 3400
*racinesnewyork.
azurewebsites.net*

With French roots, Racines NY brings a new meaning to bistro fare. Another fave of the Condé Nast crowd, who come to enjoy a glass of one of their natural wines with an elegantly plated *pâté* or mushroom tart. Try the beautifully presented veal tartare for a change of pace from beef. The space is comfortably done up with exposed brick and tin ceilings.

5

FOOD HALLS
of distinction

---

56   **LE DISTRICT**
AT: BROOKFIELD PLACE
225 Liberty St
(on the Hudson River)
Financial District ①
+1 212 981 8588
www.ledistrict.com

Right near the 9/11 Memorial is a mecca for all that is French. Peruse mustards, breads, cheese, pâté, even a chocolate mousse bar. Restaurants on the scene include: Beaubourg serving proper French classics; L'Appart the Michelin-rated intimate 28-seat boîte; at Le Bar toast a cocktail with Wall Street workers.

57   **BERG'N**
899 Bergen St
(betw Classon and
Franklin Ave)
Crown Heights, Brooklyn
+1 718 857 2337
www.bergn.com

Not just a massive Brooklyn beer hall but four foodie reasons to trek over: Mighty Quinn's BBQ (brisket and great fries); Landhaus (four burgers supreme); Lumpia Shack (build your own bowl Filipino style); and Dub Pies (dishes out mini pot pies with creative fillings). Long communal tables rule, along with a full bar.

58   **CHELSEA MARKET**
75 Ninth Avenue
(betw 15th and 16th St)
Chelsea ⑤
+1 212 652 2121
www.chelseamarket.com

Near the High Line, this market offers a taste of many worlds. The Filling Station offers infused olive oils, vinegars and salts. Corkbuzz wine bar has tasting classes. Bowery Kitchen has every culinary tool on the planet. Events include concerts, Sunday Suppers, and pop-up Designer sales.

59 GREAT NORTHERN FOOD HALL

AT: GRAND CENTRAL TERMINAL

89 East 42nd St (betw Vanderbilt & Park Ave)
Midtown ⑥
+1 646 568 4020
www.great
northernfood.com

International chef Claus Meyer has taken over a section of Grand Central to showcase his Nordic fare. Pop in for coffee, pastry, *smørrebrød* (pretty open-faced sandwich), porridge, or smoothie. Or linger with a cocktail and a Danish Dog, made with sausage, spiced ketchup, mustard, remoulade, red onion, pickled cucumber and crispy shallots on a freshly baked potato bun.

60 URBANSPACE VANDERBILT

Vanderbilt Avenue (at E 45th St)
Midtown East ⑥
+1 646 747 0810
www.urbanspacenyc.com

This is a great spot to get a taste of many of NYC's famed restaurants, all in one spot. Try tacos from La Palapa, pizza from Roberta's, fried chicken from Delaney Chicken, and finish with a sweet from Ovenly, camping out at one of their communal picnic tables. Right across from Grand Central.

56 LE DISTRICT

5 cool
ITALIAN RESTAURANTS

---

61 CASA APICII

62 West 9th St
(betw 5th and 6th Ave)
Greenwich Village ④
+1 212 353 8400
www.casaapicii.com

Situated on the garden level of a huge townhouse, the modern dining room with mid-century feel is opulently decked out in crushed velvet chairs and gold atomic lighting fixtures. The food, however, is rustic and relaxed, as evidenced by their homemade pastas and seasonal vegetable dishes. Check out the cocktail annex, Bar Fortuna, upstairs.

62 CARBONE

181 Thompson St
(betw Houston and
Bleecker St)
Greenwich Village ④
+1 212 254 3000
www.carbone
newyork.com

A throwback to the classic red sauce epoch that once ruled Italian restaurants in New York. High prices reign and Frank Sinatra broadcasts loudly. No matter what you order, a sinfully creamy bowl of burrata will arrive and be ceremoniously cut with special scissors. Tough to get a dinner reservation, lunch a bit easier.

63 GNOCCO

337 East 10th St
(betw Ave A and B)
East Village ④
+1 212 677 1913
www.gnocco.com

Simple Italian fare, located across from Tompkins Square Park. Named for the fried dough puffs that you get with prosciutto and salami in Modena, is also its excellent namesake dish. Fifteen styles of pizzas are great for sharing. Ideally located off Ave B's line up of bars, with the most appealing backyard patio in summer.

64 EMILIO'S BALLATO

55 East Houston St
(betw Mulberry and Mott)
Nolita ③
+1 212 274 8881

Faded artistic walls with haphazardly-strewn photos of former clientele welcome you to Godfather-style Italian. Known for attracting celebrities (including a recent visit by Barack Obama and his daughter) it's also known for owner Emilio Vitolo, a man with personality, who likes to interact with guests. The menu is pure southern Italian, so get the meatballs.

65 LILIA

567 Union Avenue
(at North 10th St)
Williamsburg ⑨
+1 718 576 3095
www.lilianewyork.com

Missy Robbins, known for her pasta and original sauces, is at the helm of this former auto-body shop that's been transformed into a gray-and-beige retreat. Try her Squash-Filled Ravioli with hazelnuts and sage or the more daring Spaghetti with anchovies and caramelized onions — you will not want the meal to end. The adjoining cafe serves coffee, switches to sandwiches and gelato, then a cocktail bar at 5 pm.

The 5 best places for
PIZZA

---

66 BLEECKER STREET PIZZA

69 Seventh Avenue South (at Bleecker St) Greenwich Village ④
+1 212 924 4466
www.bleeckerstreetpizza.com

The hole-in-the-wall atmosphere should not deter you from sampling pizza here. The plain cheese slice with perfectly marbled mozzarella and sauce is a New York archetype. Another favorite: the Nonna Maria with homemade marinara, fresh mozzarella and basil. Open till 5 am Friday thru Sunday. They also offer wine and beer.

67 JULIANA'S

19 Old Fulton St (betw Water and Front St) Dumbo ⑩
+1 718 596 6700
www.julianaspizza.com

Home of the original, hand-built, blazingly-hot coal oven, Juliana's is the come-back-to-life Grimaldi's, one of NY's most famous pizza places. Deliciously crispy and airy thin crusts still reign here, adorned with nice homemade toppings. Grimaldi's, around the corner, and Juliana's are locked in a stiff competition, so go and try both to see for yourself.

68 ROBERTA'S

261 Moore St (betw
White and Bogart St)
Bushwick, Bklyn ⑨
+1 718 417 1118
www.robertaspizza.com

Accompanied by rock music from their in-house radio station you can enjoy a pizza that's become a global brand. One of the earliest pioneers in Bushwick, they've set up picnic tables, and a tiki bar behind grafitti'd cinder block facade. Try the Famous Original with tomato, mozzarella, caciocavallo, and parmigiano cheeses, with oregano and chili. Less mobbed at lunch.

69 EMMY SQUARED

364 Grand St
(at S 1st St)
Williamsburg ⑨
+1 718 360 4535
www.pizzalovesemily.com

Detroit-style-pizza is served here, which means a soft, crunchy, not-too-thick crust, with cheese baked right into it. A beloved cilantro mint ranch dressing from their debut restaurant Emily's comes into play here on the signature pie, the Emmy, with mozzarella, banana peppers, slivered onions and a bowl of tangy marinara for dipping.

70 PAULIE GEE'S

60 Greenpoint Avenue
(betw West and
Franklin St)
Greenpoint, Bklyn ⑨
+1 347 987 3747
www.pauliegee.com

Reading the Paulie Gee menu is a joy in itself – a sampling of the pizza names: Ricotta Be Kiddin' Me, Feel Like Bacon Love, Anise and Anephew, and Simply Red. The part-warehouse, part-farmhouse space boasts rustic wooden tables with a huge tiled-brick oven imported from Italy. Many vegetarian/vegan options grace the menu.

5 best spots for slurping
OYSTERS

---

71 TERROIR TRIBECA

24 Harrison St
(betw Greenwich
and Hudson St)
Tribeca ③
+1 212 625 9463
www.wineisterroir.com

At Terroir, you can not only indulge on dollar oysters during happy hour (4 to 6 pm) but you can treat yourself to a lovingly-curated wine list by the inimitable Paul Grieco to pair them with. Communal high top tables encourage mingling, while exposed brick walls lend a relaxed vibe.

72 THE JOHN DORY OYSTER BAR

1196 Broadway
(at W 29th St)
Nomad ⑤
+1 212 792 9000
www.thejohndory.com

Arguably, one of the best oyster settings in New York is in the Ace Hotel, which lies on a stretch of Broadway where old gritty wholesale stores pleasantly collide with an infusion of cool. You'll be presented with a choice of six oysters, three from each coast, and a wealth of other raw bar items to choose from.

73 LONG HALL AT PIER A

22 Battery Place
(on the Hudson river)
Battery Park City ①
+1 212 785 0153
www.piera.com

This is the place to go when you want to enjoy an old-world draft beer in a space several blocks long right on the river. It's a high-spirited scene on the tip of Manhattan. Oysters, raw clams, lobster and shrimp make up the raw bar platters.

74 SEL RROSE

1 Delancey St
(at Bowery)
Lower East Side ③
+1 212 226 2510
www.selrrose.com

An adorable, hipster kind of place with artsy, crumbling walls. They carry an excellent oyster selection from some out-of-the-ordinary spots, which changes daily. Some of the creamiest, and delicate oysters we've ever sampled. Their cocktails are also very refreshing and not-too-sweet. They put tables out on the sidewalk, allowing you to truly soak up the energy of NYC.

75 ZADIE'S OYSTER ROOM

413 East 12th St
(betw 1st Ave and Ave A)
East Village ④
+1 646 602 1300
www.zadies
oysterroom.com

A long bar and slew of rustic high top tables set the scene for this quaint oyster mélange. Oysters are served every which way (raw, steamed, broiled, fried, pickled, poached) topped with prosciutto and ginger and vermouth, inside this watering hole by chef Marco Canora. Sparkling rosés, ciders and fortified wines complete the picture.

72 THE JOHN DORY OYSTER BAR

5 *great tastes of*
ASIA

---

76   NYONYA
199 Grand St (betw
Mott and Mulberry St)
Chinatown ③
+1 212 334 3669
www.ilovenyonya.com

One of the few great Malaysian restaurants
in town with a huge menu. Not exactly
comfy but the focus is squarely on their
hot and spicy dishes: *Nasi Lamak* (coconut
rice), Phad Thai, the homemade *Roti Canai*,
an all-time-favorite crispy pancake with
hot and spicy curry dipping sauce.

77   TIM HO WAN USA
85 Fourth Avenue
(at 10th St)
East Village ④
+1 212 228 2800
www.timhowanusa.com

This famed Hong Kong-based chain has
finally made it to America onto this New
York corner. Specializing in dim sum
served day and night. You can eat sitting
down or standing up at the bar in a
minimally decorated room. A busy place
that took off since its opening in 2016.

78   JEEPNEY
201 First Avenue
(betw 12th and 13th St)
East Village ④
+1 212 533 4121
www.jeepneynyc.com

Fifties nostalgia and lifesize pinups
grace the space. Eat with your hands
feasts can be had, as well as a trove of
Filipino Gastropub specialties like balut
(a fertilized duck egg), pig ear tacos, and
more tame offerings like the their burger
with Filipino flair. Exceptional cocktails
also in play here.

79 CHOP-SHOP

254 Tenth Avenue
(betw 24th and 25th St)
Chelsea ⑤
+1 212 820 0333
www.chop-shop.co

Get a dose of classic pan-Asian dishes done to perfection. Small bites include assorted summer rolls, lamb or vegetable dumplings, and rack of ribs. Noodles and rice dishes also factor in. The space has a zen, industrial feel with whitewashed brick walls, and pine stools. Backyard dining during warmer months.

80 OIJI

119 First Avenue (betw
7th St and St Marks Pl)
East Village ④
+1 646 767 9050
www.oijinyc.com

Co-owned by two chefs who worked at Bouley and Gramercy Tavern. This team has developed a menu of modern Korean food highlighted by fermented flavors particular to its cuisine. Housed in a minimalist sexy space, the food also makes a beautiful statement – the beef tartare studded with flowers, greens, and mustard seeds is almost too pretty to eat. Korean flavors work themselves into the cocktails as well.

5 spots with extraordinary
TAKE OUT

---

81 **BRODO**
200 First Avenue
(at E 12th St)
East Village ④
+1 646 602 1300
www.brodo.com

The take out window attached to upscale Hearth restaurant offers a 'hot' new concept. They offer only sipping broths and soups at Brodo (Italian for broth) in celebration of broth's inherent curative qualities. Broth is served in cups for you to sip as you would a coffee. Locations are popping up everywhere.

82 **LA ESQUINA**
114 Kenmare St
(at Lafayette St)
Nolita ③
+1 646 613 7100

Market-fresh Mexican food from a spot that every downtown New Yorker recognizes: the cool triangle building along Kenmare where food can be had from: the taqueria (sliced rib eye), the brasserie (*costillas de res* – slow roasted beef short ribs) and the café (*los waffles*).

83 **CAFÉ HABANA**
17 Prince St
(at Elizabeth St)
Nolita ③
+1 212 625 2001
www.cafehabana.com

This very popular, tight Cuban eatery is known for their delectable Mexican grilled corn or their Habana Cuban sandwich – a citrus-marinated roast pork, with Swiss cheese, chipotle mayonnaise, and pickle. Next door, the Habana-To-Go has the same menu, packed to go.

84 DORADO TACOS

28 East 12th St
(betw University Pl
and 5th Ave)
Greenwich Village ④
+1 212 627 0900
www.doradotacos.com

A counter service Mexican eatery specializing in Baja-style fish tacos in a tiny space overlooking the New York University student hustle and bustle on University Place. Tacos also come with steak, chicken, shrimp, chorizo, and vegetarian choices. Wash it all down with a Mexican beer, to stay authentic.

85 'WICHCRAFT

601 West 26th St
(at 11th Ave)
Chelsea ⑤
+1 212 780 0577
www.wichcraft.com

Celebrity chef Tom Collichio's take on the sandwich. Breakfast sandwiches are available throughout the day for those hankering a melty egg 'n' cheese. Pressed paninis oozing with Gruyère and Cuban-style pork or kale compete with more healthful combinations, like tuna with fennel and tapenade, for your attention. Many locations around Manhattan.

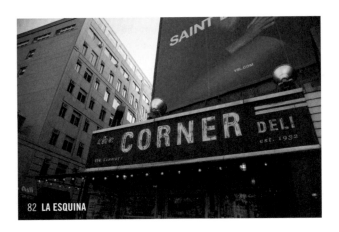

82 LA ESQUINA

A political journalist's
TOP 5 EATERIES

86 **LE COU COU**
138 Lafayette St
(at Howard St)
Soho ②
+1 212 271 4252
www.lecoucou.com

Refined and French and the talk-of-the-town inside the New York French community. With a wink to long gone Manhattan institution Lutece, Chef Daniel Rose (of La Bourse et La Vie in Paris) goes back to the cuisine's roots. Enjoy your meal in an exquisitely proportioned and well designed space, with just the right touch of rusticity.

87 **LA BOUCHERIE**
99 Seventh Avenue South
(at Grove St)
West Village ④
+1 212 837 1616
www.boucherie.nyc

Two floor bistro with lots of dry-aged steaks and classic French cuisine and a bar 'that's heavy on absinthe'. The in-house butcher makes this resto focus heavy on the meat: dry-aged New York strip, a *filet mignon*. But they also serve *Moules à la Normande*. Opened by a former chef of Pastis.

88 ATLA

372 Lafayette St
(at Great Jones St)
East Village ④
+1 646 837 6464
www.atlanyc.com

Run by the Michelin chef who owns Cosme, this place is the fast casual outlet for his imaginative, contemporary Mexican bites. You can 'join the feast' at any time of the day with their fresh selection of small plates. Try the chicken enchiladas and quail egg meatballs. Especially good for weekday lunch.

89 GLASSERIE

95 Commercial St
(betw Manhattan Ave
and Box St)
Greenpoint, Brooklyn
+1 718 389 0640
www.glasserienyc.com

Somewhat isolated location but the trek is worth it: eat under the glass ceiled courtyard in this 1860's building of formerly the Greenpoint Glass Works. Hip (clientele), Mediterranean (food) and industrial (atmosphere). Bonus: the building sits at the edge of that New York phenomenon: gentrification. Try lamb tartare with chopped olives.

90 BALTHAZAR

80 Spring St
(at Crosby St)
Soho ②
+1 212 965 1414
www.balthazarny.com

The best French brasserie in the city – period. Fifteen years ago we discovered this restaurant and we've been coming back ever since. Nothing has changed – in a good way. Just order the steak frites, like 200 other guests do every day, their fries are legendary. Go late at night for a fun scene.

5 *places to satisfy a*
SWEET TOOTH

---

91 **AMPLE HILLS CREAMERY**
AT: BUBBY'S HIGH LINE
73 Gansevoort St
(betw Greenwich
and Washington St)
Meatpacking District ④
+1 646 590 1288
www.amplehills.com

Brooklyn's favorite ice cream shop now has a spot in Meatpacking. Made with hormone-free cream from grass fed cows. Flavors are whimsical, irresistible mixes. The Ooey Gooey Butter Cake adds hunks of St. Louis-style cake to its vanilla. For sweet/savory lovers, The Munchies throws a realm of snacks into its signature pretzel-infused ice cream – crackers, potato chips, mini M&Ms.

92 **ICE & VICE**
221 East Broadway
(at Clinton St)
Lower East Side ③
+1 646 678 3687
www.iceandvice.com

Handcrafted ice cream, sorbet, and yogurt in the most sophisticated array of flavors: some quite surprising but all excellent. Pickles Of The Caribbean gets a kick of an adult beverage: rum, coconut, and pickled-pineapple jam. Movie Night supplies the gamut of movie snacks all in one bite: buttered popcorn, toasted raisins and dark chocolate.

93   RING DING BAR

AT: DUANE PARK PATISSERIE
179 Duane St
(betw Greenwich
and Hudson St)
TriBeCa ③
www.ringdingbar.com

Ring dings, once merely a mass-marketed grocery snack, have been revolutionized in this establishment. The brainchild of Madeline Lanciani, who is one of TV's *Chopped* champions, has taken the formula of cake the size of a hockey puck, and filled it with fancy creams (Nutella, strawberry cheesecake), and covered it in glazes galore (chocolate, matcha, pistachio).

94   SPOT DESSERT BAR

13 St Marks Place
(betw 2nd and 3rd Ave)
East Village ④
+1 212 677 5670
www.spotdessert
shoppe.com

Iron Chef Ian Kittichai, has a knack for creating unique, whimsical desserts. Take the Matcha Lava cake, which is served warm, with an oozing green tea ganache inside. Or the Harvest, which is delivered to your table disguised as a potted plant, whose 'dirt' is oreo crumbs topping a raspberry sorbet.

95   POPBAR

5 Carmine St
(at 6th Ave)
Greenwich Village ④
+1 212 255 4874
www.pop-bar.com

When you're on the go, it's nice to have something you can eat and walk with. Enter Popbar, with gourmet gelato – made more fun on a stick. Choose your flavor and then decide if you want to dip it in chocolate, caramel corn, crushed waffle cone, or pistachios. Sorbet and yogurt pops too.

The 5 best
CONTINENTAL
BRASSERIES

---

96 THE DUTCH
131 Sullivan St
(at Prince St)
Soho ②
+1 212 677 6200
www.thedutchnyc.com

On a cozy Soho corner, the Dutch is a lively spot where folks gather early and late. Oysters, and other raw bar selections, are a big part of the success. They have a nice roster of meat entrees, and a spectacular, albeit pricey, wine list. End your meal with one of the homebaked pies.

97 MINETTA TAVERN
113 MacDougal St
(betw Bleecker
and W 3rd St)
Greenwich Village ④
+1 212 475 3850
www.minettatavernny.com

A restaurant with a long history reimagined by restaurateur Keith McNally. Almost impossible to get a reservation, it's best to plan a late night supper at the bar. Their burger wins best in New York again and again, falling into the decadent category. Celebs may be spotted here.

98 JULE'S BISTRO
65 St Marks Place
(betw 1st and 2nd Ave)
East Village ④
+1 212 477 5560
www.julesbistro.com

Classic French bistro food plus live jazz plus expat waiters equals a tiny taste of Paris in New York. Enjoy the classics here as you cozy up with fellow music enthusiasts. The kitchen stays open late, there's no cover charge, and free Wi-Fi. Friday, Saturday, Sunday brunch is available in addition to dinner.

99 BLAUE GANS

139 Duane St
(betw Church St
and West Broadway)
TriBeCa ③
+1 212 571 8880
www.blauegans.com

A nicely proportioned room with poster art covering its walls, this Austrian spot serves casual fare in the style of a German *Wirtshaus* by one of NY's top chefs. Mingle with neighborhood families and people from the art world to enjoy classic *Schnitzel* (or one with mushrooms, bacon and herbed *Spätzle*).

100 LE PARISIEN BISTROT

163 East 33rd St (betw
3rd and Lexington Ave)
Murray Hill ⑥
+1 212 889 5489
www.leparisiennyc.com

Small, quaint and *très romantic*: Le Parisien is the perfect intimate neighborhood bistro for a date night. The menu features French comfort food like escargot, mussels, trout, onion soup and crème brûlée, and of course some great wines. A nice place to linger. It's especially popular for brunch.

96 THE DUTCH

5 places to stop at while
GALLERY HOPPING

---

101 SANT AMBROEUS

265 Lafayette St
(at Prince St)
Soho ②
+1 212 966 2770
www.santambroeus.com

The original Sant Ambroeus pasticceria
and confetteria opened its doors in Milan
in 1936. The concept was brought to New
York and translated to modern times, but
the Milanese authenticity remains. The
Soho outlet attracts an artist clientele
with signature Italian dishes like *vitello
tonnato*, *cotoletta alla milanese* and *risotti*.

102 COOKSHOP

156 Tenth Avenue
(at 20th St)
Chelsea ⑤
+1 212 924 4440
www.cookshopny.com

This energetic, greenmarket-driven hot
spot near the High Line is a perfect place
to gird yourself up for gallery hopping
in the Chelsea neighborhood. It can get
pretty crowded here: everyone loves the
uncomplicated American food (breakfast,
brunch, lunch and dinner) and the great
seating outside along 10th Ave. Book
ahead.

103 RUSS & DAUGHTERS CAFE

127 Orchard St
(at Allen St)
Lower East Side ③
+1 212 475 4880
*www.russand
daughters.com*

Russ & Daughters, a New York institution known for serving the best fish in town (caviar, lox, herring) plus classic Jewish specialties like *knishes* and potato *latkes*, opened in 1914. After 100 years they expanded with Russ & Daughters Cafe where you can sit down and nosh away. Considered one of the best restaurants in NYC.

104 BOTTINO

246 Tenth Avenue
(at 24th St)
Chelsea ⑤
+1 212 206 6766
www.bottinonyc.com

Near the High Line you'll find this art world staple: a very elegant place offering Tuscan dishes and boutique wines. Try to get seated at the comfy banquette with your back against the wall of wines, or choose a table outside in the beautiful garden out back. We like the *tagliata* (seared sliced steak).

105 TÍA POL

205 Tenth Ave
(at W 22nd St)
Chelsea ⑤
+1 212 675 8805
www.tiapol.com

Rustic and absolutely tiny, this tapas bar takes it up a few notches with traditional Basque dishes. Perfect for a pitstop and light bite at the bar. They are known for their crispy croquettes, which vary daily, and the Spanish-only wine list. Try the lamb skewers and the *patatas bravas*.

5

VEGETARIAN

hotspots

---

106 ABCV

38 East 19th St
(betw Park Ave S
and Broadway)
Gramercy ⑤
+1 212 475 5829
www.abchome.com

Chef Jean-Georges Vongerichten is expanding his abc empire to include one focused exclusively on vegetables. The decor is funky and fresh, in their inimitable style, with pops of chartreuse. Open for breakfast, lunch and dinner, feast on hearty soups, kabocha squash dip, ancient grain pilaf, and noodle dishes.

107 ROUGE TOMATE

126 West 18th St
(betw 6th and 7th Ave)
Chelsea ⑤
+1 646 395 3978
*www.rougetomate
chelsea.com*

Known for their elaborate and creative vegetable dishes, as well as their extensive, desirable wine list by sommelier Pascaline Lepeltier. This spot is housed in a space that was once a carriage house. Sedate and earthy, enjoy dinner or just pop in for a glass of wine and healthy bite.

108 DIRT CANDY

86 Allen St
(betw Grand
and Broome St)
Lower East Side ③
+1 212 228 7732
www.dirtcandynyc.com

Chef Amanda Cohen became famous for creating artistic vegetable dishes with the first, tiny outlet of Dirt Candy. Now in a larger airy space downtown, she is able to accommodate her fans. Fun dishes like the super-crunchy, battered Korean fried broccoli can make anyone become a vegetable lover.

109 **BLACK BARN**

19 East 26th St (betw
Madison and 5th Ave)
Nomad ⑤
+1 212 265-5959
*www.blackbarn
restaurant.com*

This restaurant, run by a former Waldorf
Astoria chef, is as large as an actual barn
with a sophisticated interior. Salads here
are enormous. The Garden section of
the menu focuses squarely on vegetable
entrees, like the curried cauliflower steak,
and the pickled/roasted heirloom carrots.

110 **NIX**

72 University Place
(betw W 10th
and 11th St)
Greenwich Village ④
+1 212 498 9393
www.nixny.com

This place went veggie all the way and
offers some unexpected combinations.
The space is chill, with little unnecessary
adornment, the focus is on the food. Start
with a dip or two, as the bread here is
heavenly. Then switch to small dishes to
share like the burnt broccoli, with white
cheddar, hazelnuts, and chili.

110 NIX

5 faves from a
NEW YORK FOODIE

111 DINNERTABLE

206 Avenue A
(betw 12th and 13th St)
East Village ④

A 20-seat spot that has you thinking you just landed in the home of a talented chef – and in a way you have. Enter through the sliding back door at The Garret, and plant yourself at the bar for unbridled personal attention, and to witness the Japanese-influenced American dishes being prepared. Order six or more dishes to share. We loved the beef tartare, and shrimp crudo.

112 FUSCO

43 East 20th St
(betw Park and
Broadway)
Gramercy ⑤
+1 212 777 5314
www.fusconewyork.com

Celebrity chef Scott Conant, known for his imaginative pastas and artistically presented dishes adds his personal touch to this jewel of a space. Two strategies: eat at the bar in front and rub elbows and mingle with other foodies. The dining room in the back is for more formal pursuits and tastings. Great wine list too.

113 EL QUINTO PINO

401 West 24th St
(betw 9th and 10th Ave)
Chelsea ⑤
+1 212 206 6900
www.elquintopinonyc.com

A true Spanish tapas bar. Divided into 2 spaces, the bar area is perfect for stopping by for a bite and enjoying a glass of wine, and the dining room is great for extended feasting. Do try their *bocadillos*, which are sandwiches supreme like the Bocadillo de Calamar, a flash-fried squid po' boy.

114 WALLFLOWER

235 West 12th St
(at Greenwich Ave
Greenwich Village ④
+1 646 682 9842
www.wallflowernyc.com

A little bar in front announces the adorableness of this place. Enjoy meticulously crafted cocktails by Xavier Herit, former head bartender at Daniel, while tapping your fingers along to his convivial playlists. On the dining side, the menu has a 4-course 'let us cook for you' option at 80 dollars. Late night snacks available.

115 JAMES BEARD HOUSE DINNERS

167 West 12th St
(betw 6th and 7th Ave)
Greenwich Village ④
+1 212 675 4984
www.jamesbeard.org

Hosting only the best chefs from around the US, James Beard House is a wonderful spot to mingle with fellow foodies. Located in Beard's actual townhouse, each meal starts with a cocktail hour where everyone squeezes into the space overlooking the backyard getting buzzed, then continues upstairs with a set menu at a series of communal tables.

5 restaurants for
SEAFOOD

116 **THE MERMAID INN**
96 Second Avenue
(betw 5th and 6th St)
East Village ④
+1 212 674 5870
www.themermaidnyc.com

Devoted to a menu of food from the sea, this buzzing, casual spot is staged simply with walls of photos. They take oystering seriously and have even developed an app to educate and help you to choose from the daily roster. Happy hour every day from 5 to 7 pm with 1 dollar oysters. Two other locations in Manhattan.

117 **TACOMBI**
AT: FONDA NOLITA
267 Elizabeth St (betw
Prince and Houston St)
Nolita ③
+1 917 727 0179
www.tacombi.com

Set up in a raw garage with skylight and its kitchen inside a VW bus, Tacombi is a spot serving home-style Mexican food with sustainable ingredients. Park yourself at one of their card tables on a metal folding chair to enjoy crispy fish tacos supreme and lip-smacking ceviches in a most festive environment.

118 **LURE FISHBAR**
142 Mercer St
(at Prince St)
Soho ②
+1 212 431 7676
www.lurefishbar.com

Housed in a space resembling a fine yacht, thereby accentuating their focus on the sea world. Though this spot has been there a while, it still attracts a cool crowd looking to sample raw bar goodies, sushi rolls, clam chowders, and perfectly executed fish entrees.

119 **FLEX MUSSELS**

154 West 13th St
(betw 5th and 6th Ave)
Greenwich Village ④
+1 212 229 0222
www.flexmussels.com

Slurp some mussels here, offered in four flavor profiles: white wine, creamy, tomato, and their exotic signature sauce. Start out with cornmeal-crusted clam strips, or fried oysters with spicy aioli for dipping. The space has a simple feel of a whited-out barn with pitched roof and farm landscape. Second location on the upper west side.

120 **SHUKO**

47 East 12th St
(betw Broadway
and University Pl)
Greenwich Village ④
+1 212 228 6088
www.shukonyc.com

Owners Nick and Jimmy both worked at legendary Masa, and have developed one of the city's best sushi tasting menus, with menu items based on what looks freshest that day, combined with exotic ingredients from far-away locales. Forgoing tradition, some of their combinations can be a little on the edge. Also known for their artisanal sakes, and cocktails.

117 TACOMBI

5 top
TASTING MENUS

---

121 AGERN
AT: GRAND CENTRAL
TERMINAL
89 East 42nd St
(at Park Ave)
Midtown ⑥
+1 646 568 4018
www.agernrestaurant.com

The brainchild of Claus Meyer, the man behind Copenhagen's Noma, considered one of the world's best restaurants, now in Grand Central Terminal with Icelandic-born Gunnar Gislason as the chef. Many of his dishes feature ingredients from Nordic realms, including the cocktails. They offer two tasting menus, one focused on meat and fish, the other mostly vegetables.

122 THE EDDY
342 East 6th St
(betw 1st and 2nd Ave)
East Village ④
+1 646 895 9884
www.theeddynyc.com

Charming and down-to-earth digs underplay the artistry and playfulness of the dishes. You might start off with house-made *lángos*, then a vegetable course, choice of main dish and side, plus dessert. Along with the nicely-priced tasting menu, you can order a tasty cocktail which will arrive in a sweet, ornamental teacup.

123 **THE MUSKET ROOM**

265 Elizabeth St (betw
Prince and Houston St)
Nolita ③
+1 212 219 0764
www.musketroom.com

A handsomely rustic dining experience
led by the talents of a New Zealand chef.
A garden out back provides many of the
greens and herbs in the dishes. The space
looks comfortably informal, but dishes
that come out are meticulously, almost
breathtakingly styled, and the flavors are
wonderfully unexpected.

124 **GABRIEL KREUTHER**

41 West 42nd St
(betw 5th and 6th Ave)
Midtown ⑥
+1 212 257 5826
www.gknyc.com

The Alsatian chef, formerly of The
Modern, is running the show here in
the most sophisticated way. The space is
divided into two sections, with a more
casual menu at the bar. For a special
night, opt for the 4-course *prix fixe* in
the main dining room, and be lovingly
treated to beautifully-styled dishes with
his signature touch.

125 **THE MODERN**

9 West 53rd St
(betw 5th and 6th Ave)
Midtown ⑥
+1 212 333 1220
www.themodernnyc.com

We love dining in The Bar Room, but if
you are looking for a meal to remember,
book a dinner in the dining room that
overlooks MoMA's sculpture garden.
Service is impeccable, along with the
artsy plates and silverware customized to
each course. Dress up. For true foodies,
book The Kitchen Table, where the chef
prepares a bespoke menu.

CAFFE REGGIO

70 PLACES
FOR A DRINK

5 places to fuel up with
COFFEE

---

126 TARALLUCCI E VINO
**15 East 18th St (betw
5th Ave and Broadway)
Union Square ⑤
+1 212 228 5400**
www.tarallucievino.net

This is a true-Italian, upscale spot, where you can drink your shot their way, standing at the counter. Iced espresso, made the proper way – by shaking, can be had, along with a full breakfast menu and pastries. It's open all day, so you can switch to wine later, or stop for a sandwich, or dinner. 3 other locations.

127 JOE COFFEE
**141 Waverly Place
(at Gay St)
West Village ④
+1 212 924 6750**
www.joenewyork.com

On one of the quaintest corners in the village are two benches where you can take in the NYC *Zeitgeist* as you relax and sip your morning Joe. The art of coffee is taken seriously here, with staff trained to be proper baristas, and where they roast their proprietary blend. 9 other locations.

128 BLUESTONE LANE
**1114 Sixth Avenue
(at W 43rd St)
Midtown ⑥
+1 212 764 0044**
www.bluestonelaneny.com

A nice pitstop on your midtown touring schedule. Located across from Bryant Park and in the courtyard of the Grace building lies this rustic departure. This Australian coffee chain offers Melbourne fare for snacking: like avocado with a tahini twist, or their P.L.A.T. (prosciutto, lettuce, avocado, and tomato).

129 BROOKLYN ROASTING COMPANY

25 Jay St (betw Plymouth and John St) Dumbo, Brooklyn ⑩
+1 718 514 2874
www.brooklyn roasting.com

Dumbo is where you'll find producers, photographers and other creatives who spend their days shooting TV shows and commercials. Get your coffee alongside them near the water in a large warehouse setting, where the beans are actually roasted. Their fair trade coffee beans are sourced from only the top coffee estates in South and Central America.

130 LA COLOMBE TORREFACTION

400 Lafayette St (at 4th St) Noho ④
+1 212 677 5834
www.lacolombe.com

In a majestic sun-filled space, sip extraordinary coffee sourced around the globe. They're known for their roasting and blends, and for being the inventors of latte on draft: a cold-pressed espresso with frothed milk served cold (also available in cans for toting). You will encounter a line, but it moves quickly. 5 other locations.

127 JOE COFFEE

5 places to sip cocktails in
L U X *setting*

---

131 **DEAR IRVING**

55 Irving Place
(betw 17th and 18th St)
Gramercy ⑤
www.dearirving.com

How could you not adore sitting in the art deco lounges surrounded by glamorous silver beads or in the Napoleonic-style room with opulent chandeliers and naughty wallpaper? Cocktails are stellar and come at the push of a bell, just like at sister lounge Raines Law Room. Try to get a seat at the gold-accented bar near the charming TomR.

132 **SWEET POLLY**

71 Sixth Avenue
(betw Flatbush Ave
and Bergen St)
Prospect Heights,
Brooklyn ⑪
+1 718 484 9600
www.sweetpollynyc.com

High, embossed gold ceilings, a gorgeous living plant wall, and sleek mirrors set the mood for its upscale clientele. Sit at the elegant white marble bar with old fashioned lamps that subtly illuminate your cocktails. Order a Dirty Martini on tap, or get the night going with a kick of caffeine in The Golden Eye.

133 CLOVER CLUB

**210 Smith St (betw
Baltic and Butler St)
Cobble Hill, Brooklyn** ⑬
+1 718 855 7939
www.cloverclubny.com

Two vibes: In the back, an elegant wood-paneled lounge with beamed mirrored ceilings mixed with Louis XIV chairs, 70s chandeliers, and a cozy fireplace. Up front, the vintage mahogany bar is where carefully prepared pre-Prohibition drinks are created: a variety of fizzes, smashes, swizzles and sours. Live jazz, and a neighborhood feeling waft through.

134 LE BOUDOIR

**135 Atlantic Avenue
(betw Henry
and Clinton St)
Brooklyn Heights,
Brooklyn** ⑩
+1 347 227 8337
www.boudoirbk.com

In a space that was once part of the Atlantic Avenue tunnel lies an opulent fantasy, styled after Marie Antionette's private rooms. Think plush red velvet booths and ornate mirrors. Enter through the bookcase door of their upstairs spot Chez Moi, for decadent cocktails like the Dauphin: absinthe, chile liqueur, almond milk, coconut, cacao nibs.

135 BLACKTAIL

AT: PIER A – HARBOR HOUSE,
2ND FLOOR
**22 Battery Place
Battery Park City** ①
+1 212 785 0153
www.blacktailnyc.com

A lush and vibrant scene inspired by 1920s Cuba, the space is decorated in dark wood, wicker, vintage posters, and tropical foliage under a stained glass ceiling. Their cocktail menu is presented as a beautifully illustrated book, which highlights the five categories of cocktails: highballs, punch, sours, old fashioned, and misc. A nice interlude all the way downtown with stellar drinks.

5 bars to meet
BANKERS

---

136 **THE BEER BAR**
AT: THE METLIFE BUILDING
200 Park Avenue
(near E 45th St)
Midtown East ⑥
+1 212 818 1222
www.patinagroup.com/
the-beer-bar

Bankers and hedge fund managers stop in here on their way to Grand Central where they catch the train back to Connecticut. Located outside, under the MetLife building, this convivial spot is a loud and wild scene, which escalates as the night goes on. Best spot for singles looking to make a score.

137 **STONE STREET TAVERN**
52 Stone St
(betw Hanover Sq
and Coenties Alley)
Financial District ①
+1 212 785 5658
www.stonestreet
tavernnyc.com

Stone Street Tavern backs onto one of the few pedestrian streets in the city and is lined with fun places to meet and greet. Every restaurant on this block has communal picnic tables set up – and it's where Wall Streeters like to let loose and party. Historically, this was the first paved street in Manhattan.

138 **DORRIAN'S RED HAND**
1616 2nd Avenue
(at 84th St)
Upper East Side ⑦
+1 212 772 6660
www.dorrians-nyc.com

Red checkered table-cloths say old New York, in the most classic sense. This place attracts the preppie and finance crowd who come for the relaxed vibe and camaraderie. Tuesday nights feature karaoke, a great night to mingle, and fans young and old gather to watch the game.

139 CASA LEVER

390 Park Avenue
(at E 53rd St)
Midtown ⑥
+1 212 888 2700
www.casalever.com

Located on that part of Park Avenue which is virtually all banks, it's a place where men in suits conduct serious business while downing elegant Italian dishes. The bar at the front is slightly more casual, with same clientele enjoying Martinis, exceptional wines by the glass, and small bites. Cool architecture and original Warhol portraits.

140 CIPRIANI CLUB 55

55 Wall St
(betw William
and Hanover St)
Financial District ①
+1 646 300 8163
www.cipriani.com

Regulars from Deutsche Bank and Goldman Sachs head here to elegantly unwind. Dine on the gorgeous outdoor terrace with palm trees and imposing columns that looks out right onto Wall Street, or in the library-style room with exotic wood paneling. Go early evening and order a Bellini, of course.

140 CIPRIANI CLUB 55

5 great spots for
INTELLECTUALS

---

141 THE SCRATCHER
209 East 5th St
(at Cooper Sq)
East Village ④
+1 212 477 0030

The Scratcher, Irish slang for 'going to bed', is the place where journos of *The New York Observer* drink after work and where the young and hip mix in a chill Irish environment located behind an unassuming façade. Starts quiet but fills up later with locals. Good selection of beers. Live music Sundays.

142 THE HALF KING
505 West 23rd St
(at 10th Ave)
Chelsea ⑤
+1 212 462 4300
www.thehalfking.com

Founded in 2000 by a couple of journalists and a filmmaker, this casual hangout attracts writers, artists, and editors to their weekly Monday readings, photojournalist slideshows and Magazine Night. Author of *The Perfect Storm*, owner Sebastian Junger's latest topic of interest is Tribe, exploring why humans crave belonging in small groups.

143 KGB BAR

85 East 4th St (betw
2nd Ave and Bowery)
East Village ④
+1 212 505 3360
www.kgbbar.com

KGB Bar has long serviced literary types in its red walled divey space. Regular readings have taken place here since the early 1990s. In the Red Room upstairs you can see performances, storytelling, poetry readings, with Sundays set aside for fiction read by emerging writers. Check the calendar for almost daily events.

144 THE EAR INN

326 Spring St
(betw Greenwich
and Washington St)
TriBeCa ③
+1 212 226 9060
www.earinn.com

One of the oldest bars in New York. The name comes from its famous neon sign, where part of the letter B in BAR is missing. Creative types mingle with regulars and listen to live music, which happens three nights a week, along with poetry readings and film screenings, fed by an elevated farm-to-table bar menu.

145 CAFÉ LOUP

105 West 13th St
(betw 6th and 7th Ave)
Greenwich Village ④
+1 212 255 4746
www.cafeloupnyc.com

A Village standby attracting literary types, neighborhood regulars, with a bar known as a friendly spot to engage in conversation with strangers. Fantastic bartenders, who keep the extra Martini for you in the shaker, and charming waitstaff add to this place's allure. Back in the 90s Susan Sontag and Paul Auster could be spotted here.

5 places to get
COFFEE and LINGER

---

146 MAMAN

239 Centre St (betw
Grand and Broome St)
Soho ②
+1 212 226 0700
www.mamannyc.com

The brainchild of a Michelin chef, a
mixologist, and a baker, this charming
spot is absolutely picture-perfect, as
witnessed on their Instagram page. Sit
near the open kitchen or spread out in
the pleasant back room. Known for their
tartinettes and crispy-on-the-outside-soft-
on-the-inside-cookies.

147 STUMPTOWN

30 West 8th St
(at MacDougal St)
Greenwich Village ④
+1 855 711 3385
www.stumptowncoffee.com

This location epitomizes the clean and
modern Stumptown aesthetic, with
exposed brick walls, long benches, and
an attractive parquet floor. Located on the
stretch of 8th Street that is coming back
to life with new and exciting venues, it's
a quiet space you can linger in.

148 HI-COLLAR

214 East 10th St (betw
1st and 2nd Ave)
East Village ④
+1 212 777 7018
www.hi-collar.com

A sweet, zen Japanese place inspired by
kissaten (old-school Japanese coffee shops).
Grab one of their 13 stools and try their
extra fluffy pancakes along with a coffee,
which is brewed precisely in a siphon and
served in pretty ceramic tea cups. At night
they switch their focus to sake.

149 CAFFE REGGIO

**119 MacDougal St (betw
W 3rd and Bleecker St)
Greenwich Village** ④
+1 212 475 9557
www.caffereggio.com

Where cappuccino was introduced
to America in 1927, this spot is a true
Village piece of history with its original
ornamental espresso machine preserved
on display. Its old-world atmosphere still
attracts the latest generation of creative
thinkers. Sit outside at one of the small
round tables and watch the world go by.

150 UPRIGHT BREW HOUSE

**547 Hudson St
(at Perry St)
West Village** ④
+1 212 810 9944
*www.upright
brewhouse.com*

In this case, brew refers to coffee *and* to
their selection of craft beers. There's an
outside bench here on the most pleasant
stretch of Hudson street, as well as cozy
seats behind the window inside. Solid
lattes and pastries – and brunch, dinner,
and wine if you decide to stay all day.

147 STUMPTOWN

The 5 best places to enjoy a
BEER

---

151 **ZUM SCHNEIDER NYC**
107 Avenue C
(at E 7th St)
East Village ④
+1 212 598 1098
www.zumschneider.com

A Bavarian *Bierhaus* where New Yorkers mix with German expats to enjoy 10+ German beers on tap as well as a dozen bottled beers. The space mimics an actual *Biergarten*, with arched brick walls and fake foliage. Outside seating with umbrellas is popular. They host the annual Oktoberfest along the East River (with Oompah band!).

152 **MISSION DOLORES BAR**
249 Fourth Ave (betw
Carroll and President St)
Park Slope, Brooklyn ⑬
+1 347 457 5606
www.missiondolores.com

Located inside an industrial space that was once a tire shop, it's known for being one of New York's best outdoor beer gardens. Pinball machines (a rarity in the city, strangely enough) grace a rough concrete courtyard hung with 'mug shots' of criminals. Cask beer (fresh and unpasteurized) is available, plus 20 beers on tap.

153   TØRST

615 Manhattan Avenue
(betw Nassau
and Driggs Ave)
Greenpoint, Bklyn ⑨
+1 718 389 6034
www.torstnyc.com

Opened by Jeppe Jarnit-Bjergso, a Danish brewer, and Daniel Burns, once head of Momofuku's test kitchen. The space resembles a minimalist beer lab, a mix of cool white marble and reclaimed wood panels. Beer pours from 21 taps using a specialized system ensuring your brew comes out at the correct temperature.

154   BLIND TIGER

281 Bleecker St
(at Jones St)
Greenwich Village ④
+1 212 462 4682
www.blindtiger
alehouse.com

A microbrewery stationed on the part of Bleecker street away from the upscale boutiques. Twenty-eight beers on tap compete with their bottled beer selections, which are divided into categories like Sours & Funk, and Barrel-aged, plus some really special picks. Accompany your chugging with their Grilled 5 Cheese sandwich.

155   PROLETARIAT

102 St Marks Place
(betw 1st Ave and Ave A)
East Village ④
www.proletariatny.com

For the beer pioneer. This long, narrow, 20-seat bar sits on infamous East Village's St Marks Place. They specialize in unusual craft beers from microbreweries, and the bartenders are knowledgeable about the different brews. Half pours are available, so you can try as many kinds as you like. No TVs. No sports.

5 great
OLD SCHOOL
bars

---

156 OLD TOWN BAR
**45 East 18th St
(betw Broadway
and Park Ave)
Union Square** ⑤
+1 212 529 6732
www.oldtownbar.com

Old Town is a bar set up as real bars are meant to be: a no-nonsense, no music, beer-swilling brouhaha. High ceilings create a feeling of space, mosaic tile floors are classic (as are the marble pissoirs in the men's room). Go one flight up to order one of the best burgers in town.

157 WALKER'S
**16 North Moore St
(at Varick St)
TriBeCa** ③
+1 212 941 0142
www.walkerstribeca.com

A neighborhood bar with locals and guys-in-suits-come-to-loosen-their-ties, remains a slice of this neighborhood's working-class past. Housing a well-worn bar and cool photos of Tribeca's past, this is the spot for a draft beer or whiskey and good (stiff) regular cocktails.

158 FANELLI CAFE
**94 Prince St
(at Mercer St)
Soho** ②
+1 212 226 9412

Soho, in all its fashionableness, still embraces this character-filled hold out (since 1922). Squeeze in at the bar, where you might end up talking to a leftover resident artist from the 80s, or at one of the red-and-white checkered tablecloth tables. Staff comes with NY attitude to complete the picture.

159 **MAISON PREMIERE**

298 Bedford Avenue
(betw S 1st and Grand St)
Williamsburg ⑨
+1 347 335 0446
www.maisonpremiere.com

Waiters in vests and bowties cordially maneuver in this space inspired by New Orleans circa 1890. The bar has a serious cocktail program plus 1-dollar oysters from 4 till 7 on weeknights, that attract a crowd to its lovely horseshoe-shaped marble bar. Best spot is the outdoor patio with canopy of foliage.

160 **SAUVAGE**

905 Lorimer St
(at Nassau St)
Greenpoint, Bklyn ⑨
+1 718 486 6816
www.sauvageny.com

The gorgeous etched-glass panels give this new spot an old-world homey feel. Sauvage's bar program favors cocktails made with low-proof spirits, plus their enviable collection of more than 200 artisanal small-batch liquors. Natural wines dominate the wine list with a focus on those made with ancient winemaking techniques.

156 OLD TOWN BAR

The 5 best
HOTEL *and* ROOFTOP
BARS

---

161 **KING COLE BAR**
AT: ST REGIS HOTEL
2 East 55th St (at 5th Ave)
Midtown ⑥
+1 212 339 6857
www.stregisnewyork.com/
king-cole-bar

Roam amongst the city's happy elites. Table 55 is, by legend, the most exclusive table in New York. If you reserve it be ready to spend a minimum of 2500 dollars. Here, the bags are Birkin, the faces lifted, and the bottle ordered should be Taittinger Comtes de Champagne 1075.

162 **BEMELMANS BAR**
AT: THE CARLYLE HOTEL
35 East 76th St
(at Madison Ave)
Upper East Side ⑦
+1 212 744 1600

Red jacketed waiters remind us of the long lost New York iconized by Frank Sinatra. Settle in at the bar for a night to remember, and chat up the Upper East Side clientele. Woody Allen plays on Tuesdays at this spot where live jazz dominates. Pricey cover charge after 9 pm.

163 **TEMPLE COURT**
AT: THE BEEKMAN HOTEL
5 Beekman St (betw
Park Row and Nassau St)
Financial District ①
+1 212 658 1848
www.templecourtnyc.com

One of the most astounding spaces to sip a cocktail in NYC, inside a breathtaking nine-story Victorian atrium. In this landmarked 1883 Gothic Revival building, the bar is a study in gold and green, with old-fashioned iron stools, and lighting via small lamps. Get a table and luxuriate in the comfortable opulence.

164 **GALLOW GREEN**

AT: THE MCKITTRICK HOTEL
**530 West 27th St
(betw 10th and 11th Ave)
Chelsea** ⑤
+1 212 564 1662
*www.mckittrickhotel.com/
gallow-green*

Total scene above the place famous for the immersive theater experience *Sleep No More*. Less about views and more about a lush escape from the city. Decked out in greenery and backyard patio lights in summer, dolled up like a log cabin in winter – with amazing attention to detail. Earlier is better, if you want to gain access.

165 **B BAR**

AT: THE BACCARAT HOTEL
**20 West 53rd St
(at 5th Ave)
Midtown East** ⑥
+1 866 957 5139
www.baccarathotels.com

Down the block from MoMA, B Bar is as stunningly beautiful as a palace, with elaborate namesake crystal chandeliers everywhere you look. At the bar, you may snag one of the bar stools for two (which seem to be popping up more and more). Cocktails will be elegantly presented in iconic Baccarat cut crystal glassware.

162 BEMELMANS BAR

5 places for
OENOPHILES

166 AIR'S CHAMPAGNE PARLOR

127 MacDougal St
(betw W 4th and 3rd St)
Greenwich Village ④
+1 212 420 4777
*www.airschampagne
parlor.com*

Let the sommelier guide you through the sparkling world of flavors at this champagne-only bar. It's an adorable art deco parlor with a world assortment of affordable to splurgy bottles. Deals happen at Parlor Hour (5 to 7 pm) – with three glasses of bubbly plus snacks for a fixed price with a different theme each day.

167 LOIS

98 Avenue C
(betw E 6th and 7th St)
East Village ④
+1 212 475 1400
www.loisbarnyc.com

This wine bar is the first place in NYC to only offer wine on tap. Their wines are available by the glass or the carafe, for a nice price – not bottling the wine cuts costs and the savings are passed on to you. The space is clean, modern and fresh. Try one of their healthy bites, like the avocado arepas.

168 **FIG. 19**
131 1/2 Chrystie St
(betw Broome
and Kenmare St)
Lower East Side ③
www.figurenineteen.com

Hidden behind a door at the end of an art gallery lies a cool, raw space with chandeliers and fireplace. We chose this spot to include in our oenophile roundup solely because they have prosecco on tap, and it's a place that always attracts a lively, indy, artsy crowd at all hours of the night.

169 **BROOKLYN WINERY WINE BAR**
213 North 8th St (betw
Driggs and Roebling St)
Williamsburg ⑧
+1 347 763 1506
www.bkwinery.com

One of two full-fledged winemaking facilities in NYC, Brooklyn Winery produces about 20 varieties in their picturesque space (which hosts many a wedding). Get a taste of the signature wines at the wine bar, by the glass or bottle. Flights allow you to sample 3 different varietals, like the NY State Trio, or Chardonnay 3 Ways.

170 **ALDO SOHM WINE BAR**
151 West 51st St
(betw 6th and 7th Ave)
Midtown West ⑥
+1 212 554 1143
www.aldosohm
winebar.com

This is like being in Aldo's comfortable, sleek living room. The longtime sommelier of Le Bernardin has set up shop next door, off a mall in the middle of 51st Street, offering (more) affordable wines and small plates. For something really special, be there for Aldo After Dark, when he opens his daily magnums at 9 pm.

5 *funky bars on the*
LOWER EAST SIDE

---

171 MEHANATA BULGARIAN BAR

113 Ludlow St
(betw Delancey
and Rivington St)
Lower East Side ③
+1 212 625 0981
www.mehanata.com

Gypsy music rules! Anything goes here, including the wildly popular ice cage, a refrigerated space where you put on Soviet military gear and fur hats and have two minutes to drink shots of vodka. A place to truly unwind and dance to music from the Balkans – and beyond – in a no frills setting with Bulgarians and locals.

172 MAX FISH

120 Orchard St
(betw Delancey
and Rivington St)
Lower East Side ③
+1 212 529 3959
www.maxfish.com

The illustrious red-and-blue polka dotted LES establishment bar/art gallery moved to a new location in 2014, bringing along its famous cigarette-shaped light fixture. They still show artists work and act as a haven for downtown artists, skaters, and neighbors. Follow them on Instagram.

173 HOME SWEET HOME

131 Chrystie St (betw
Broome and Delancey St)
Lower East Side ③
+1 212 226 5709
www.homesweethome bar.com

Taxidermy enthusiasts will get their fill here in this space outfitted almost like a curiosity shop. If you like to dance, you've come to the right dive bar. They've got a lounge with a dance floor and the DJs play a quirky mix of 50s-90s-swing. Dancing usually starts after 10 pm.

174 MARSHALL STACK

**66 Rivington St
(at Allen St)
Lower East Side ③
+1 212 228 4667
www.marshallstacknyc.
com**

A true LES gem that has an extra long bar with a great selection of decently-priced bottled beers. A mishmash interior of painted white brick mixes with exposed plaster and painted tin ceilings, with a 1950s-style jukebox (!) full of righteous rock tunes. Bar food, like Sliders and Tilapia Po' Boys can be had too.

175 WELCOME TO THE JOHNSON'S

**123 Rivington St (betw Norfolk and Essex St)
Lower East Side ③
+1 212 420 9911**

A dive in every sense of the word, from its sticker-covered old brown refrigerator holding 2-dollar Pabst Blue Ribbons and plastic-covered sofas. Imagine the 1970s basement of heroin addicts, complete with layers of graffiti covering every inch of the bathroom walls. They boast killer Bloody Marys and a pool table too.

172 MAX FISH

5 *great places for*
ARTISANAL COCKTAILS

176 **HOLIDAY COCKTAIL LOUNGE**
**75 St Marks Place
(betw 2nd and 3rd Ave)
East Village** ④
+1 212 777 9637
*www.holidaycocktail
lounge.nyc*

For nearly 100 years, this space attracted notables with personality (Madonna, Sinatra, Keith Richards, Iggy Pop, Allen Ginsburg, Trotsky). The recent modern-with-kitsch makeover retains a vintage feel. Cocktails are cultivated by brothers Michael and Danny Neff, who are committed to honoring its gritty, celebrity-studded past.

177 **SUFFOLK ARMS**
**269 East Houston St
(at Suffolk St)
Lower East Side** ③
+1 212 475 0400
suffolkarms.com

Giuseppe González, an outspoken veteran mixologist runs this place, which harks back to British pubs of yore. The space has some old-fashioned high-back wooden booths, and a fantastic narrow table running down the center designed for setting down drinks and mingling. Cocktails have been heavily researched and they are presented with personality, in unapologetic, NYC style.

178 ANALOGUE

**19 West 8th St (betw
5th and 6th Ave)
Greenwich Village** ④
+1 212 432 0200
www.analoguenyc.com

Enjoy your artisanal cocktail with the sounds of live Brazilian jazz in the background. The space is set up in a modern, clean style, with long leather banquettes lining one side of the room. As with most cocktail driven bars, the menu changes with the seasons, and they'll make a special concoction just for you.

179 LAZY POINT

**310 Spring St
(betw Hudson
and Greenwich St)
TriBeCa** ③
www.lazypointnyc.com

An out-of-the-way spot that's great for cocktails and late night dancing. This block hosts a few other hot spots, but this place is unassuming and cheerful with its nautical and beachy motifs. If you like tequila, try the Underhill's Tab or the Lomax Paloma made fresh with nice juices.

180 ATTABOY

**134 Eldridge St
(betw Broome
and Delancey St)
Lower East Side** ③
+1 855 877 9900

In the former Milk & Honey space, two of its former bartenders have set up a new place to sip cocktails. An expanded bar and narrow booths line the laid-back white brick space. No menu: you are invited to describe what you like. No reservations: ring the buzzer next to the steel door with "AB" to get in.

5 places to watch
FOOTBALL
(the Euro kind)

---

181 PUBLIC HOUSE
140 East 41st St
(betw Lexington
and Park Ave)
Midtown East ⑥
+1 212 682 3710
www.publichousenyc.com

Here football is religion, so you can catch all the games, all the time, live: Champions League, Premier League, La Liga, and more. The space is vast, with high ceilings and room to spread out. Giant TVs sit in four areas behind the bar. Mingle at happy hour with a crowd of young professionals.

182 BXL CAFÉ
125 West 43rd St (betw
6th Ave and Broadway)
Midtown ⑥
+1 212 768 0200
www.bxlrestaurants.com

Jules is the quintessential restaurant/ bar owner – don't think we've ever seen him in a bad mood. This is where you can escape from the craziness of Times Square, and nurse yourself with football and food: Belgian beer and all-you-can-eat *moules frites*. In Flatiron try his BXL Zoute on 50 W 22nd Street.

183 BONSIGNOUR
35 Jane St
(at 8th Ave)
West Village ④
+1 212 229 9700

Admittedly not a real football place unless you come during the European or World football cups when you can watch TV on the street with fellow fans. Hot & cold sandwiches, paninis and a fridge stacked with San Pellegrino's. Sit on the bench in front and you're in Old Europe.

184 SWEETWATER SOCIAL

643 Broadway
(at Bleecker St)
Noho ④
+1 212 253 0477
www.drinksweetwater.com

A subterranean lounge, not-your-average football-watching bar — it's considerably more haute than hooligan. We don't think football-obsessed visitors will mind. The drink menu is cleverly charted out on a New York subway map with each cocktail alluding to a subway stop. Foosball tables and an 80s vibe encourage interaction.

185 MOLLY'S PUB & RESTAURANT SHEBEEN

287 Third Avenue (betw
E 22nd and 23rd St)
Gramercy ⑤
+1 212 889 3361
www.mollysshebeen.com

A more low-key, civilized place to watch a match among fellow fans, whether they're rooting for your team or not. Molly's is a true Irish shebeen with sawdust on the floor and multiple Guinness taps manned by skilled pourers. The menu offers fantastic versions of Irish favorites like shepherd's pie, along with exceptional American bar faves.

183 BONSIGNOUR

5 places with a
PERSONALITY
all their own

---

186 **SID GOLD'S REQUEST ROOM**
165 West 26th St
(betw 6th and 7th Ave)
Chelsea ⑤
+1 212 229 1948
www.sidgolds.com

Glitzy, as in Las Vegas, with kitschy 1950s barware and memorabilia. Karaoke singing goes on in the back around a grand piano. Pianist Joe McGinty, formerly of the Psychedelic Furs, is often on hand and can play whatever you request.

187 **THE UNCOMMONS**
230 Thompson St (betw
Bleecker and W 3rd St)
Greenwich Village ④
+1 646 543 9215
www.uncommonsnyc.com

For those who love to play games, literally. Inside is an entire wall stacked with over 1200 board games (Monopoly, Backgammon, Risk, and other obscure titles). For 5 dollars you can go in and play all the games you want. Coffee, tea – plus beer, wine, and cider.

188 **BROOKLYN BOWL**
61 Wythe Avenue (betw
N 11th and 12th St)
Williamsburg ⑨
+1 718 963 3369
www.brooklynbowl.com

The triple threat: a music venue, bar, and upscale sixteen lane bowling-alley – which sits right next to where live acts, like Guns N' Roses and Elvis Costello, have played. Acts include the latest indy bands, novelty shows, and a weekly spin by DJ Questlove. Great fried chicken supplied by a NYC favorite, Blue Ribbon.

189 MARIE'S CRISIS

**59 Grove St (betw
7th Ave S and Bleecker)
West-Village** ④
+1 212 243 9323

A show tune sing-along place filled with enthusiastic, diehard fans. Mostly gay men (though all theater lovers come and are welcome) surround a piano in an underground spot, and beautifully belt out one show tune after the other, while drinking from plastic cups. It's a joyful spot that dates back to the early 1900s.

190 THE STONEWALL INN

**53 Christopher St
(at 7th Ave)
Greenwich Village** ④
+1 212 488 2705
*www.thestonewallinn
nyc.com*

The site of the riots in 1969, and now a National Landmark. A rite of passage for many gay men, it's a short walk from Washington Square Park – you'll recognize it by its iconic arched red brick facade, neon sign, and rainbow flags waving. Afternoon drinking encouraged with 2-for-1 drinks between 2 and 7.30 pm.

190 THE STONEWALL INN

5 hipster bars not to miss in
BROOKLYN

---

191 TOOKER ALLEY
793 Washington Avenue
(betw St John
and Lincoln Pl)
Prospect Heights,
Brooklyn ⑪
+1 347 955 4743
www.tookeralley.com

Down the street from the Brooklyn Museum of Art is a bar where craft cocktails are taken seriously, but presented quite humorously, with poetry and stories to entertain you on the menu. Counterculture is celebrated here: jazz (on the soundtrack), and a general bohemian attitude. Sample your favorite creative interpretation of the Manhattan.

192 MONTANA'S TRAILHOUSE
445 Troutman St
(betw St Nicholas
and Cypress Ave)
Bushwick, Brooklyn
+1 917 966 1666
*www.montanas
trailhouse.com*

One step into Montana's and you've entered a quirky shack in the woods. This former auto repair shop has been refitted with wood salvaged from a Kentucky barn. The front room is full of Americana, and has a wall of windows with stools where you can park yourself. Cocktails use well-sourced ingredients, like jams and homemade syrups.

193 LOT 45

411 Troutman St
(betw Wychoff and
St Nicholas Ave)
Bushwick, Brooklyn
+1 347 505 9155
www.lot45bushwick.com

Get up and dance. A big industrial space scattered with a fun mix of mismatched couches, exposed brick and fancy chandeliers, located on the street in the epicenter of Bushwick's street art. The patio outside serves a French Algerian street-style menu. Nice cocktails. Check the calendar for music and art events.

194 FORREST POINT

970 Flushing Avenue
(betw Bogart St
and Morgan Ave)
Bushwick, Brooklyn
+1 718 366 2742
www.forrestpoint.com

Once a gas station, now a colorful spot covered in murals, with a playful backyard complete with a jumble of swing sets, stools made of tree stumps, and festive strings of lights. A casual spot where neighbors show up with their dogs. Order the Milk Punch, a milk-based complicated cocktail based on recipes from early America.

195 JUPITER DISCO

1237 Flushing Avenue
(betw Gardner Ave
and Ingraham St)
Bushwick, Brooklyn
www.jupiterdisco.com

A bar inspired by the one in *Star Wars*, this one is loaded with amusingly-dated audio equipment and sci-fi accoutrement. Drink menus scroll on TVs behind the bar in the style of 80s computer screens. Every cocktail and draft beer is a limited edition, so as things run out they're crossed out on the menu.

70 PLACES TO SHOP

———

The 5 best stores for
BOOKWORMS

---

196 RIZZOLI BOOKSTORE

1133 Broadway (betw
W 25th and 26th St)
Nomad ⑤
+1 212 759 2424
www.rizzoliusa.com

One of the latest high-end additions to the 'hood', this bookstore is known for their superb selection of illustrated books on beautiful topics: art, design, gardening, cooking, and more. Some books in Italian, French, and Spanish, plus many European magazines and newspapers. Celebrated authors do readings here, so do check the calendar.

197 THE STRAND

828 Broadway
(at E 12th St)
Greenwich Village ④
+1 212 473 1452
www.strandbooks.com

Advertised as 18 miles of books, they offer services unlike any other bookstore, and can curate a library to match both your personality *and* decor. Their special first editions are the ones that collectors drool over. It's an easy way to kill an afternoon, strolling the aisles or thumbing through the cheap books set up on the sidewalk outside.

197 THE STRAND

199 THREE LIVES & COMPANY

198 GREENLIGHT

686 Fulton St
(at S Portland Ave)
Fort Greene,
Brooklyn ⑩
+1 718 246 0200
greenlightbookstore.com

Hooray for the independent bookseller. This forward-thinker was welcomed into the neighborhood with open arms. In-store events: on Saturday mornings kids get story time; evenings host more thoughtful conversations with leading authors. Some of their bigger book launches take place at BAM, and include the famous – like John Cleese, Elvis Costello, Lena Dunham, and Neil Gaiman.

199 THREE LIVES & COMPANY

154 West 10th St
(at Waverly Pl)
Greenwich Village ④
+1 212 741 2069
www.threelives.com

A cozy independent bookstore that's part of what makes the Village so quaint. On this corner since 1983, they are sure now to stay in the neighborhood. Locals have learned to rely on owner Toby Cox's recommendations and come to the store regularly to share thoughts on books they have read.

200 MCNALLY JACKSON

52 Prince St
(betw Lafayette
and Mulberry St)
Nolita ③
+1 212 274 1160
www.mcnallyjackson.com

This independent bookseller has fans: nightly events draw crowds to meet with sought-after authors. They stay on the cutting edge of the digital age, self-publishing 700 books a month – and you can make a carry-able version to take with you with their on-site printer, or create a special edition as a gift. Café on the premises offers java and Wi-Fi.

The 5 best
ART BOOK STORES

201 METROPOLITAN MUSEUM OF ART BOOKSTORE
1000 Fifth Avenue
(at E 82nd St)
Midtown ⑥
+1 212 535 7710
www.metmuseum.org

After you've perused all the wondrous art at the museum, there's a craving to bring a piece of that experience home. Prints, posters, jewelry, note cards, all await you, amongst the incomparable collection of art books on the scene. It's the spot where you can purchase one of their own published works, to remind you of the exhibit you saw – or a past exhibit – for years to come.

202 MAST BOOKS
66 Avenue A
(at E 5th St)
East Village ④
+1 646 370 1114
www.mastbooks.com

Independently-owned and one of New York's no-nonsense art book stores, Mast Books has a wonderful selection of out-of-print and secondhand books, periodicals, and rare editions. You'll find a great selection on fine art, photography, design, fashion and cinema, along with some literary fiction and poetry. They buy and sell, carry artists' catalogues, and new editions too.

203 URSUS

50 East 78th St (betw
Park and Madison Ave)
Upper East Side ⑦
+1 212 772 8787
www.ursusbooks.com

You could get lost in this sanctum of art books, intriguing to collectors and beginning art lovers alike. Ursus is an institution with an unmatched collection of art books from five centuries, including the most rare illustrated books, catalogues and prints. Check the website to see the breadth and depth of their inventory.

204 192 BOOKS

192 Tenth Avenue
(at W 21st St)
Chelsea ⑤
+1 212 255 4022
www.192books.com

Operated by the Paula Cooper Gallery, known for its minimalist and conceptual art support, this store carries a well-curated selection of books on art and photography as well as literary fiction, history, and biography. They host readings, events and signing sessions, plus a weekly story hour for children on Wednesdays at 11 am.

205 PRINTED MATTER

231 Eleventh Avenue
(at W 26th St)
Chelsea ⑤
+1 212 925 0325
www.printedmatter.org

Founded by Sol LeWitt and several other artists, this nonprofit bookstore specializes in serious and political artists' books, zines, posters, and prints, including an extensive selection of out-of-print material. Their goal is to preserve and provide insight into publications made and distributed by artists. Ongoing events include zine releases, exhibitions, and book announcements.

5 places to shop with your
GIRLFRIENDS

---

206 MARYAM NASSIR ZADEH

123 Norfolk St
(betw Delancey
and Rivington St)
Lower East Side ③
+1 212 673 6405
www.mnzstore.com

Maryam Nassir Zadeh, the shop's owner and designer, is known to New Yorkers for her meticulous style. The shoes and apparel are a minimalist's dream and tailored to perfection for the office. There is an aura of old world chic and fashion insiders flock here for Zadeh's latest designs.

207 THE REFORMATION

23 Howard St (betw
Crosby and Lafayette St)
Soho ②
+1 212 510 8455
www.thereformation.com

Being naked is the number one sustainable option – after that, anything from this store. They design and manufacture their clothing using only the most sustainable materials, upcycled fabrics from deadstocks and repurposed vintage clothing. Other locations on the LES.

208 ARTISTS & FLEAS IN CHELSEA MARKET

88 Tenth Avenue
(at W 15th St)
Chelsea ⑤
+1 917 488 0044
www.artistsandfleas.com

This is a place to interact with artists and find little gems. Browse over 30 independent designers, foodie stalls and small eateries. The market holds a great range of goods by independent designers and shop owners ranging from art, music, vintage, handbags to handmade jewelry.

209 BABEL FAIR

260 Elizabeth St (betw
Prince and Houston St)
Nolita ③
+1 646 360 3685
www.babelfair.com

For those who flit around in flowy
dresses with original style, head here
for a selection of brands you won't see
anywhere else – from far-flung places
(Brazil, Japan, Argentina, +) specially
chosen by founder Erica Kiang. Think
bodysuits, jumpsuits, leather jackets,
trenches, and statement pieces.

210 BHLDN & ANTHROPOLOGIE

1230 Third Avenue
(betw E 71st and 72nd St)
Upper East Side ⑦
+1 212 288 1940
www.anthropologie.com

Each Anthropologie location impresses
with its decor alone. This unique lifestyle
brand is a cult favorite among the boho-
chic crowd looking for a one-stop shop.
You will find a well-curated selection of
colorful apparel and accessories, only the
most covetable books, and home decor.
This location takes appointments for
brides-to-be and entourage looking for
romantic wedding attire.

210 BHLDN & ANTHROPOLOGIE

5 places to bump into a
DOWNTOWN IT GIRL

---

211 **OPENING CEREMONY**

35 Howard St (betw
Broadway and Crosby St)
Soho ②
+1 212 219 2688
www.opening
ceremony.com

All the fashion pieces you see in glossy magazines and on celebrities come together in one place. The slight European feel of the shop is due to their many brands from abroad. Collaboration with the hippest designers attracts models, fashion bloggers and only the coolest girls in the city.

212 **CLOAK & DAGGER**

334 East 9th St
(betw E 1st and 2nd Ave)
East Village ④
+1 212 673 0500
www.cloakanddagger
nyc.com

The uniqueness of this store lies in the 1960s cool-girl vibe and inviting mix of vintage and new. As a designer herself, the owner has a great eye and carries brands that reflect the store's aesthetic. Browsing is fun and employees are always well dressed, armed with smart style advice.

213 **ANINE BING**

330 Bleecker St
(betw W 10th and
Christopher St)
West Village ④
+1 646 590 1161
www.aninebing.com

Anine Bing arrived on the scene with a big splash. Hunting for a perfect pair of jeans, trendy boots or a leather jacket becomes easier when everything in the store is *au courant* and cut to perfection. The store carries all the pieces you need to get you through more than one season.

214 CREATURES OF COMFORT

205 Mulberry St (betw
Kenmare and Spring St)
Nolita ③
+1 212 925 1005
www.creatures
ofcomfort.us

This is one of the many stores that captures the epitome of New York. It is a lifestyle brand that many chic working women shop for work and play. Known for collaborating with world famous fashion influencers, the apparel and accessories are made well and are far from a fad – pieces here can stand the test of time.

215 LOVE ONLY

434 East 9th St
(betw 1st Ave and Ave A)
East Village ④
+1 917 280 0649

This is a place where you come to shop when you want to stand out from the crowd. The selection is curated by its owner into a color schemed haven for local and overseas independent designers. It is very rock and roll babe meets model-off-duty. Shop for gorgeous dresses, coats and one-of-a-kind gift ideas.

5 cool designer shops for
HIM and HER

216 HELMUT LANG

38 Gansevoort St
(betw Greenwich and
Hudson St)
Meatpacking District ④
+1 212 242 4165
www.helmutlang.com

Peruse the NYC homestead of a minimalist-deconstructivist collection, in the heart of Meatpacking. Under newly appointed *Dazed and Confused*'s Editor-in-Chief Isabella Burley's lead, expect a return to the brand's roots, including a special collection with Hood By Air designer Shayne Oliver.

217 IF SOHO

94 Grand St (betw
Mercer and Greene St)
Soho ②
+1 212 334 4964
www.ifsohonewyork.com

A store devoted to the urbane desires and needs of the cultured, art-minded dresser. Staff here are keyed into the genre, and will help craft your original look – if you look the part. Think of brands like Comme des Garçons, Dries van Noten, Guidi, Yohji Yamamoto, Ann Demeulemeester, and Haider Ackermann.

218 A.P.C.

131 Mercer St (betw
Spring and Prince St)
Soho ②
+1 212 966 9685
usonline.apc.fr

Check into the French brand – sporting
cult denim and a soulful, modernist
viewpoint. Enjoy the aesthetic of architect
Laurent Deroo, who has been the vision
behind their store's appeal. Devoted fans
can always get a new pair of jeans for half-
price when they turn in their used pair. For
discounted overstock items from previous
season, head to the Perry St location.

219 ACNE STUDIOS

33 Greene St
(at Grand St)
Soho ②
+1 212 334 8345
www.acnestudios.com

This store allows you to take in a little at
a time. Small, styled rooms that feel like
someone's carefully stocked closet make
up the space, letting their Stockholm-
minimalist aesthetic pervade. Their stuff
is just so wearable, with much longevity.
Though known for their denim, this store
encases so much more.

220 RICK OWENS

30 Howard St
(at Crosby St)
Soho ②
+1 212 627 7222
www.rickowens.eu

The spot for the international designer's
line is at this flagship in NYC, showcased
in a raw, cement-dominated space, with
a staff who engage. The 8000-sq-ft space
carries everything – from his collections
on the runway, DRKSHDW staples, Adidas
footwear, leather accessories, to his wife
Michele Lamy's Hunrod jewelry line.

The 5 best places to
SHOP LIKE
A NEW YORKER

---

221 OAK

28 Bond St
(betw Lafayette St
and Bowery)
Noho ④
+1 646 682 7899
www.oaknyc.com

It is no myth that most New Yorkers wear black on all occasions and there are shops willing to deliver with mostly, black, grey, and white selections — OAK is one of them. The shop is pleasing to the eye and very fashion forward. Stop in to find what you are missing. They carry men's, women's, and accessories.

222 SPACE NINETY 8 (UO)

98 North 6th St (betw
Wythe and Berry St)
Williamsburg ⑨
+1 718 599 0209
www.uospaces.com

Urban Outfitters has provided three floors of shopping and relaxation that capture the spirit of the neighborhood. The brand firmly believes in the artist and has included many Brooklyn-made goods. Spend your afternoon shopping the hipster and quirky items you come to UO for, then grab a drink with a view on the rooftop.

223 3X1 DENIM

15 Mercer St (betw
Canal and Grand St)
Soho ②
+1 212 391 6969
www.3x1.us

In the world of premium denim 3x1 is a guru workshop with a special concept for creating custom-made jeans. If you fancy yourself a denim collector or someone who likes a precise fit why would you not go here? It is one of those secret and cool New York places. They are experts.

224 DOVER STREET MARKET

160 Lexington Avenue
(betw E 30th and 31st St)
Murray Hill ⑥
+1 646 837 7750
www.doverstreet
market.com

Fashion enthusiasts of unique and even one-of-a-kind items come here to spend money. You will be awed by the floors and floors of high-end designer goods. From top to bottom: the space, the clothes, the art installations and the staff are gorgeous and stylish. And there is a cafe to take a break from it all.

225 MADEWELL

115 Fifth Avenue
(at E 19th St)
Flatiron ⑤
+1 212 228 5172
stores.madewell.com

Every girl on-the-go knows the value of a comfortable pair of jeans and a tank top. Madewell aims to please. The brand is known for the latest in trends but not the crazy high prices. Editors love shopping here. Stop by to pick up your next pair of summer sandals or a soft dress that you can enjoy for years to come.

5 Brooklyn shops for the
FASHION FORWARD

---

226 BIRD

203 Grand St
(betw Bedford Ave
and Driggs St)
Williamsburg ⑨
+1 718 388 1655
www.birdbrooklyn.com

This boutique has become a Brooklyn staple. Brooklynites want more of what the store sells, and they do not want to run to Manhattan to get it. As a former buyer for Barneys, Bird's owner has a sophisticated eye and, lucky for Brooklyn residents, the brand keeps expanding and collaborating with designers.

227 SWORDS-SMITH

98 South 4th St
(betw Berry St
and Bedford Ave)
Williamsburg ⑨
+1 347 599 2969
www.swords-smith.com

If you find yourself in the mood for some retail therapy, browse through this well-curated selection of independent designers. The indie shop is pleasing to the eye and has a flow that allows you to shop and not feel crowded. They carry clean straight silhouettes, each item designed as a conversation piece that ups your cool status.

228 CATBIRD

219 Bedford Avenue
(betw N 4th and 5th St)
Williamsburg ⑨
+1 718 599 3457
www.catbirdnyc.com

The definition of the word 'pretty', this beloved boutique stocks a collection of delicate indie jewelry meant to be personally expressed in stacks and layers, plus a selective assortment of beauty and home products. Materials are ethically sourced, with jewelry-making happening in a studio on the premises.

229 SINCERELY TOMMY

343 Tompkins Avenue
(betw Madison and
Monroe St)
Bedford Stuyvesant
+1 718 484 8484
www.sincerelytommy.com

Step into this minimalist's dream shop for emerging local and global womenswear and lifestyle brands – picture loose silhouettes that go with the flow. The store's layout is roomy and makes it a pleasure to shop. Plus there is a coffee counter serving fair trade coffees.

230 FRONT GENERAL STORE

143 Front St
(betw Pearl and Jay St)
Dumbo ⑩
+1 646 573 0123
www.frontgeneralstore.com

The Dumbo area is popular for photo-ops alone, and this vintage shop is the icing on the cake. It is packed with goodies of all kinds: gorgeous Native American jewelry, hats, jeans jackets, boots, pottery – the list goes on. Stumble in and walk out wearing something truly dapper and in vogue.

228 CATBIRD

230 FRONT GENERAL STORE

5

VINTAGE SHOPS

for cool finds

---

231 COBBLESTONES
314 East 9th St
(betw 1st and 2nd Ave)
East Village ④
+1 212 673 5372

Step off the street and into a time capsule. This shop has been in the East Village for years and is filled to the brim with vintage goodies. Celebrities and stylists love to shop here but they would never tell. The owner has a unique style of her own, a bright soul with extensive knowledge for vintage fashion.

232 DUO NYC
337 East 9th St
(betw 1st and 2nd Ave)
East Village ④
+1 212 777 7044
www.duonyc.com

You will find cool jewelry made by local designers, must-have jeans, natural fibers with simple silhouettes and organic beauty. Whatever you decide to purchase will quickly become your go-to item for many years to come. The owners are two sisters whose style is something to be admired.

233 STOCK VINTAGE

143 East 13th St
(betw 3rd and 4th Ave)
East Village ④
+1 212 505 2505
www.stockvintagenyc.com

When movie sets find themselves in need of vintage, Stock Vintage is one of their go-to shops. Enjoy the very organized layout and interesting façade in the bohemian East Village. They specialize in American workwear and you can also discover some hard-to-find military clothing and accessories. A must see.

234 BEACON'S CLOSET

10 West 13th St
(betw 5th and 6th Ave)
Greenwich Village ④
+1 917 261 4863
www.beaconscloset.com

A staple among stylish New Yorkers strapped for cash. If you enjoy vintage hunting you will be pleased with the packed variety of selection. New Yorkers and international shoppers all mingle here hoping to find a gem or two. You can buy, sell and trade vintage, as well as second-hand, in all its locations.

235 SHAREEN VINTAGE

13 West 17th St
(betw 5th and 6th Ave)
Flatiron ⑤
+1 212 206 1644
www.shareen.com

Unless you read about it or were keyed in by a fellow vintage aficionado, Shareen is so hidden you would just pass it by. That is because it's located on the second floor of a loft-like warehouse building. If you see a dress hanging off a fire escape, that means they're open. How New York! The vintage bride should have this romantic place at the top of her wedding dress shopping list.

5 stores for **ATHLETIC** and **OUTDOOR** pursuits

236 **BANDIER**

164 Fifth Avenue (betw
W 21st and 22nd St)
Flatiron ⑤
+1 646 360 3345
www.bandier.com

Fitness-meets-fashion in this airy loft of a store. In this flagship, browse their collection of brightly printed leggings, spiffy footwear, super socks, and totes for hauling all your gear. Upstairs is Studio B where you can sign up for a fitness class and show off your new outfit. Ladies only.

237 **ROOTS**

228 Elizabeth St (betw
Prince and Houston St)
Nolita ③
+1 646 833 7417
www.roots.com

Roots is a Canadian brand that makes long-lasting quality clothing and accessories for playing in the rough outdoors and for being extra cozy indoors. Customers come in search of warm sweatshirts, sweatpants, athletic wear, socks, and leather goods. If you are a fan of having a distinct outdoor look, this shop is for you.

238 **FILSON NYC**

40 Great Jones St
(betw Lafayette St
and Bowery)
Noho ④
+1 212 457 3121
www.filson.com

Filson is the steadfast brand that speaks to outdoorsy, masculine guys with only the highest aesthetic standards. Explore their inventory of signature backpacks, toiletry kits, leather accessories, and outerwear – all made in uncompromising style with field-tested materials and workmanship.

239 **PARAGON**

867 Broadway
(at E 18th St)
Flatiron ⑤
+1 212 255 8889 or
+1 800 961 3030
www.paragonsports.com

This store boasts four massive floors packed with gear for literally every kind of sport – keeping in sync with the seasons. Runners rejoice – like Cinderella, you can find the perfect sneaker that fits, plus adjust your running gait, just suit up with different pairs in the store and run on a treadmill for videotaped analysis.

240 **PATAGONIA**

72 Greene St (betw
Spring and Broome St)
Soho ②
+1 212 334 5213
www.patagonia.com

Yes, it's a chain, but a nice one. They allow you to take in damaged goods for repair, host environmental groups' film screenings, and on Sunday there's free yoga. If they don't stock the item you absolutely must have, they will find it at one of their other locations and deliver it to you via bike messenger that day.

238 **FILSON NYC**

5 men's stores for those with
INDIVIDUAL STYLE

---

241 SATURDAYS NYC

31 Crosby St (betw
Grand and Broome St)
Soho ②
+1 212 966 7875
www.saturdaysnyc.com

For those into riding waves, get a fix of surf life here. Start with a signature-blend espresso, browse surfboards, men's attire, books, then make your way to the backyard – where you might meet fellow surfers and swap tales. The style is laid-back, with a bent for cotton and natural fabrics in soft colors.

242 THE LODGE

220 East 10th St
(betw 1st and 2nd Ave)
East Village ④
+1 212 777 0350
www.lodgegoods.com

The accessory obsessed gentleman will find this small shop is big on heritage style must-haves. From luxurious handmade leather goods to grooming staples, you will start browsing as soon you step in. It seems as if every inch of the store is designed to hold a special item. The service is friendly and the whiskey is plentiful.

243 ALIFE RIVINGTON CLUB

158 Rivington St (betw
Suffolk and Clinton St)
Lower East Side ③
+1 212 432 7200
www.alife.nyc

Ring a bell to get into a gentlemanly
boutique stocked with limited-run
covetable sneakers and cool streetwear,
like Alexander Wang's collection for
Adidas. This trio of shops are exclusively
for the serious sneaker and streetwear
collectors – the suave setting might
inspire you to switch up your closet.

244 IDOL BROOKLYN

101 Metropolitan
Avenue (betw Wythe
and Berry St)
Williamsburg ⑨
+1 718 599 4365
www.idolbrooklyn.com

Stepping into this well-lit and organized
space is a pleasure. They are known
for a fashion-forward selection and
knowledgeable customer service. Think
minimalist with lots of black and olive
pieces and classic plaids. Why not make
it a pleasant afternoon by revamping your
closet with cutting-edge designs and a
proper Williamsburg brunch afterwards.

245 FREEMAN'S SPORTING CLUB

8 Rivington St (betw
Bowery and Chrystie St)
Lower East Side ③
+1 212 256 1309
www.sportingclub.com

For a taste of an old-fashioned shopping
experience – where you can get a tailored
suit or a sharp haircut and shave all in
one spot, step into Freeman's. You can get
fitted for a custom sportcoat, or browse
their selection of casual wear, manly
accessories, and grooming products.

5 one-of-a-kind
GIFTS & HOME
shops

---

246 PINK OLIVE
439 East 9th St
(betw 1st Ave and Ave A)
East Village ④
+1 212 780 0036
www.pinkolive.com

Escape into this magical shop for all your gift-giving needs. You will find artsy and smart greeting cards, art for your walls, baby gifts, home decor, candy, books. Bring your creative teen along. The service is a breath of fresh air, they honestly love helping you find what you need.

247 LES ATELIERS COURBET
175 Mott St
(betw Broome
and Kenmare St)
Nolita ③
+1 212 226 7378
www.ateliercourbet.com

Exquisite old world craftsmanship is the theme at this gallery/shop which showcases collectible pieces in home accessories, along with furniture and lighting. The space, once a carriage house, is now handsomely outfitted with double height windows, and elements of antiquity preserved.

248 ABC CARPET AND HOME
888 Broadway
(betw E 18th and 19th St)
Union Square ⑤
+1 212 473 3000
www.abchome.com

Six floors encompassing a style all their own, this store is a shopping wonderland. Browse through their eco mix of handmade and rough-hewn tabletop stuff, eclectic barware, handmade designer jewelry, unique gifts, and luxurious bedding. Make sure to hit the basement level. Peace.

249 MOMA DESIGN STORE

81 Spring St
(at Crosby St)
Soho ②
+1 646 613 1367
www.store.moma.org

This downtown post of the famous design store is chock-full of design-y stuff, with a bit more room than its midtown cousin. You'll find the same quirky, useful household tools, plus books, bags, and their usual scarves. New stuff includes an iPhone camera lens sets, a super cool tree tent, and a levitating speaker.

250 THE FUTURE PERFECT

55 Great Jones St (betw
Lafayette and Bowery)
Noho ④
+1 212 473 2500
www.thefutureperfect.com

The store that started out in Williamsburg championing unknown designers and artists takes its collection to Noho. See the next wave of design here with their interesting mix of handsome and also unusual items. Home accessories include pillows and throws, vases, planters, terrariums, and decorative items.

250 THE FUTURE PERFECT

5 meccas for
SHOES *and* SNEAKERS

---

251 NO.6

8 Centre Market Place
(betw Grand and
Broome St)
Nolita ③
+1 212 226 5759
www.no6store.com

Stop here for a cool selection of clogs in spiffy colors and designs with both wedge and stacked heel (even in bootie styles), plus super-wearable pumps with splayed wide heels and slingbacks in pop colors. This shop was founded by Karin Bereson, a savvy vintage collector/stylist, so the clothes here are special too.

252 KITH

644 Broadway (betw
Bleecker and Bond St)
Noho ④
+1 646 648 6285
www.kith.com

Keyed into the world of NYC street style, Queens-born owner and footwear designer Ronnie Fieg is known for his clever collaborations with major brands. The sneakers here are of the limited-edition kind, providing culture-influencing product that his fan base expects.

253 CHRISTIAN LOUBOUTIN

59 Horatio St
(betw Greenwich
and Hudson St)
West Village ④
+1 212 255 1910
www.christian
louboutin.com

Everyone knows about the red soles, but shopping this famous shoe designer at the Horatio location feels very hidden and exclusive. The outside blends in with the West Village neighborhood but once you walk in, get ready to be wowed. If you are in the market for an expensive shoe, this is the place to be.

254 FLIGHT CLUB

812 Broadway
(at W 11th St)
Greenwich Village ④
+1 888 937 8020
www.flightclub.com

More for the fashion crowd than serious runners. Sneaker fanatics and collectors can search through walls and walls of name-brand sneakers new, vintage and lusted-after. Consignment rules, so sizes are random, upping the thrill of the hunt. Opposite the sneakers is a wall of baseball caps, so you can coordinate your purchase.

255 THE SHOE BOX

123 Fifth Avenue
(betw E 19th and 20th St)
Flatiron ⑤
+1 646 490 6759
www.shoptheshoebox.com

Ladies, you've hit the jackpot here with the best designer shoes of the season all in one spot. View the latest from McQueen, Sam Edelman, No. 21, plus their eponymous brand. Go from affordable to wish-list styles, with a conscientious staff who are there for you. Two locations in Manhattan.

254 FLIGHT CLUB

5 stores for
ACCESSORIES
head to toe

---

256 JJ HAT CENTER

310 Fifth Avenue
(betw W 31st and 32nd St)
Midtown ⑥
+1 212 239 4368
www.jjhatcenter.com

Introduce something classic and swanky into your life. This hat shop is the oldest in New York, boasting a space and set of loyal customers epitomizing a world of class. Service is top notch, everyone working here is a pro, so you and your hat will be taken care of for life, including steaming and shaping.

257 FABULOUS FANNY'S

335 East 9th St
(betw 1st and 2nd Ave)
East Village ④
+1 212 533 0637
www.fabulousfannys.com

If you have to wear glasses, be different. Whether your preferred style of frame is classic or spiffy, Fabulous Fanny's is like a mini capsule of styles from different eras. Movie sets rely on them for their collection of frames that go back to the 1700s. A dying breed in New York, you would be wise to go experience it.

258 LA PETITE COQUETTE

51 University Place
(betw E 9th and 10th St)
Greenwich Village ④
+1 212 473 2478
www.thelittleflirt.com

Your undergarments need love too. Shop Le Petite Coquette for sexy and sensual bras, panties, slips, hosiery and even sleepwear. The delightful shop resembles a pin-up girl's boudoir. Enjoy the great service and its luxury merchandise designed for grown-up women. This is an investment you won't regret.

259 BITE BEAUTY LIP LAB

174 Prince St
(betw Sullivan and
Thompson St)
Soho ②
+1 646 484 6111
bitebeauty.com

The brainy creators of Bite have set up a lab for anyone who enjoys a good tube of lipstick. Beauty addicts and those who struggle to find their perfect match come here to find beauty bliss. The space is welcoming and creative, mirroring a bakery environment. So witty! Go find your personal shade of red lipstick.

260 FINE & DANDY

445 West 49th St
(betw 9th and 10th Ave)
Hell's Kitchen ⑥
+1 212 247 4847
*www.fineanddandy
shop.com*

Spruce up your wardrobe with a custom shirt, pocket square, neckerchief, cufflinks, or suspenders from the fine collection at this dapper gentlemen's clothing store. The quaint shop belongs to the era of the well-dressed-man-about-town. It is very cosmopolitan and you will walk out accessorized to the nines. Swell!

5 lifestyle
CONCEPT SPACES

---

261 **THE APARTMENT BY THE LINE**

76 Greene St (betw Broome and Spring St)
Soho ②
+1 917 460 7196
www.theline.com

Enter a space that's set up to look like someone's – a world traveler with exquisite taste – lived-in apartment. All is for sale, including the items that fill the walk-in closet and every perfectly-positioned prop. Its 3rd floor location hosts a lush diamond-tufted velvet couch, and kitchen with hand-blown glass chandeliers.

262 **STORY**

144 Tenth Avenue
(at W 19th St)
Chelsea ⑤
+1 212 242 4853
www.thisisstory.com

Every few months Story totally reinvents itself with a new theme. A concept from 2016, 'The F-Word' was interpreted to mean Feminist, Fair trade, and Fatherhood, with designer items to go with each. Past themes: Have Fun (emojis, ping pong), Disrupt (tech), Remember When ('90s nostalgia).

263 KINFOLK 90

90 Wythe Avenue
(at N 11th St)
Williamsburg ⑨
+1 347 799 2946
www.kinfolklife.com

A trio of friends from Japan, LA, and NYC have created a space that's not only a retail store, but an event/performance space, with a hidden bar inside a super-groovy, repurposed-wood geodesic dome. Shop their line of cool, casual clothing for guys, with well-made, laid-back accessories, and vintage sci-fi books.

264 WHISPER EDITIONS

8 Fulton St (betw
South and Front St)
Financial District ①
www.whispereditions.com

Whisper Editions teams up with selected photographers, jewelry designers, artists, apothecaries, and other creatives to create limited editions of their goods. Founded by a photo editor at *Vanity Fair*, the store reflects her discerning eye, and has a natural style all its own.

265 CANAL STREET MARKET

265 Canal St
(betw Broadway
and Lafayette St)
Soho ②
+1 646 694 1655
www.canalstreet.market

Once a carriage house, now a retail market and food hall on the edge of Chinatown. Search through 24 booths set up in an airy 12.000-sq-ft space housing local artisans work and cool brands. In the house: edgy blankets from La Douzaine, totes from Yul, home accessories from American Design Club.

FLATIRON BUILDING

25 BUILDINGS TO ADMIRE

5 buildings with
HISTORY

---

266 FEDERAL HALL

26 Wall St
(cnr of Broad St)
Financial District ①
+1 212 825 6990
www.nps.gov/feha

Just steps away from the New York Stock Exchange, Federal Hall marks the spot that was once America's first Capitol. Its columns loom majestically over Wall Street, with a statue of George Washington out front. Explore the stunning Greek Revival architecture inside, along with historical exhibitions. Free.

267 FRAUNCES TAVERN

54 Pearl St
(at Broad St)
Financial District ①
+1 212 425 1778
www.frauncestavern
museum.org

This landmarked 1719 building was HQ to George Washington during the American Revolution. Originally built by Henry Holt, who taught dance and held balls in the space. Take a guided tour to be taken back to colonial times. Or, take in history at the still operating tavern.

268 LIBRARY OF BRONX COMMUNITY COLLEGE

2155 University Avenue
The Bronx
+1 718 289 5100
www.bcc.cuny.edu

A beautiful example of a Beaux Arts building designed by architect Stanford White, featuring the breathtaking dome of the Gould Memorial Library, outfitted in marble, mosaics, and Tiffany glass. At its rear, The Hall of Fame offers views of the Harlem River and busts of great Americans.

269 TRINITY CHURCH

75 Broadway (at Wall St)
Financial District ①
+1 212 602 0800
www.trinitywallstreet.org

It's amusing to think that Trinity Church was once the tallest structure in NYC. Its Gothic Revival architecture dates back to 1846, with surrounding cemetery dating back much further, housing the grave of Alexander Hamilton, America's first Secretary of the Treasury (and current Broadway musical smash). Concerts are held regularly in St. Paul's Chapel.

270 GRAND CENTRAL STATION

89 East 42nd St
(at Park Ave)
Midtown ⑥
+1 212 340 2583
www.grandcentral
terminal.com

Opened in 1913, the main train hub in NYC harkens back to a time of sophisticated travel. Meet at the Clock, which is centered below the Sky Ceiling, an opulent astronomical mural. Downstairs, in front of the Oyster Bar, is the famous whisper wall, from which two people can communicate via whisper from opposite archways.

267 FRAUNCES TAVERN

5 impressive
EARLY SKYSCRAPERS

---

271 **CHRYSLER BUILDING**

405 Lexington Avenue
(at E 42nd St)
Midtown ⑥
www.nycgo.com/attracti-
ons/chrysler-building

New York's most adored skyscraper, because of its elegant and sublime Art Deco detailing, inside and out. Famous for its stylized eagles at the corners of its arched crown (even prettier at night). Gargoyles match the medieval ones on Paris' Notre Dame. Pop into the lobby to admire its luxe mix of marble, and the ceiling mural.

272 **WOOLWORTH BUILDING**

233 Broadway (betw
Barclay St and Park Pl)
Financial District ①
+1 203 966 9663
www.woolworthtours.com

Our personal favorite because of its ornate façade, a resemblance to many European Gothic cathedrals. The building was commissioned by F.W. Woolworth, owner of the famous five-and-dime chain, and designed by architect Cass Gilbert in 1913. To get inside, sign up for a tour or head to the restaurant, The Wooly Public.

273 FLATIRON BUILDING

175 Fifth Avenue
(at E 23rd St)
Flatiron ⑤

Named the Flatiron, due to its shape resembling a clothes iron, the wedge-shaped steel-framed building was completed in 1902. Residents were skeptical that the building could remain standing, considering its width of only 6 ½ feet (1,95 meters) at its narrowest point. Adjacent to Madison Square Park.

274 ROCKEFELLER CENTER

45 Rockefeller Plaza
Midtown ⑥
+1 212 332 6868
www.rockefeller
center.com

Nineteen Art-Deco-style buildings, whose main building, '30 Rock', houses NBC studios. Walk by in the early morning to witness the scene of *Today Show* fans vying to get on the air. For views, head to The Observation Deck or the bar in the Rainbow Room. Winter brings the annual Christmas tree and ice skating rink.

275 WILLIAMSBURG SAVINGS BANK TOWER

1 Hanson Place
(at Flatbush Ave)
Downtown Brooklyn ⑩

Brooklyn's high point is often referred to as its 'most phallic building'. The four-sided clock tower was a bank but is now a luxury condo. The ground floor still retains the vaulted bank hall as an event space, and the winter home to the Brooklyn Flea which sells vintage clothing, collectibles, and crafts by local designers.

5 must-see
MODERN
buildings

---

276 COURTYARD ENTRANCE OF THE BLOOMBERG TOWER

731 Lexington Avenue
(betw E 58th and 59th St)
Midtown East ⑥

Home of the company founded by former NYC mayor Michael Bloomberg. The entrance sits in a 7-story elliptical courtyard, whose effects get more dramatic when lit up at night. Restaurant Le Cirque beckons on the ground floor servicing the celebs who live in the million dollar condos in the 55-story tower above.

277 NEW YORK BY GEHRY

8 Spruce St
(betw Nassau
and William St)
Financial District ①
+1 212 877 2220
www.newyorkbygehry.com

World-renowned architect Frank Gehry's eye-catching undulating tower. It stands next to the iconic Woolworth Building and at 76 stories it's one of tallest residential skyscrapers in the world. Clad in stainless steel it catches the light and its curves allow windows to project for unparalleled views.

278 VIA 57

625 West 57th St
(betw 11th Ave and
West Side Hwy)
Hell's Kitchen ⑥
+1 646 630 7917
www.via57west.com

On the Hudson River sits a dramatic pyramid, with a trapezoid cut-out housing a courtyard with trees, a totally new example of residential living in NYC. Architect Bjarke Ingels incorporated many eco-conscious ideas into his design. Best viewed from one of the city's tour boats.

279 NEW YORK TIMES BUILDING

620 Eighth Avenue
(betw W 40th and 41st St)
Midtown ⑥
+1 718 923 8640
*www.newyorktimes
building.com*

Opposite the depressing Port Authority Bus Terminal lies a new modern classic housing the offices of *The New York Times*. Designed by Renzo Piano, it bears a 100-foot-long name of the newspaper along the 8th Avenue façade and has many built-in green features, including the ceramic tubes that create a skin over the building.

280 ONE57

157 West 57th St
Midtown ⑥
+1 212 570 1700
www.one57.co

This striking 1005-foot-tall glass tower is a good example of the building frenzy along 57th Street, making this *the* new upscale residential stretch. It's marketed as 'above and beyond' because of its views over Central Park, and it's also one of the buildings that ignited a very New York-ish discussion over loss of sunlight over the southern part of the park.

280 ONE57

5 *places to*
ADMIRE THE VIEW

---

281 EMPIRE STATE BUILDING
338–350 Fifth Avenue
(betw 33rd and 34th St)
Midtown ⑥
www.esbnyc.com

On top of perhaps the world's most iconic New York skyscraper, you'll get the view of views. There are observatories on the 86th floor (main deck) and the 102nd floor (top deck). To avoid the lines, pay for an Express Pass. Buy tickets from salesmen in yellow or green jackets outside the building or online.

282 ONE WORLD TRADE CENTER
285 Fulton St
(at West St)
Financial District ①
+1 844 696 1776
www.oneworld
observatory.com

Go 104 floors to reach the top of the tallest skyscraper in the Western hemisphere where you'll get panoramic views – as long as it's not cloudy. On the way up, elevators clad in high res screens will show you how NYC went from fields to a small village to the metropolis it is today. Buy tickets online to save time.

283 BELVEDERE CASTLE
AT: CENTRAL PARK
Mid-Park at 79th St
Midtown ⑥
+1 212 772 0288
www.centralparknyc.org

For views of a more bucolic nature, position yourself inside the middle of Central Park. This castle, designed by one of the park's famous architects, has two balconies providing views of the reservoir, the south lawns and beyond. You can borrow binoculars from the nature observatory located inside the castle.

284 WYTHE HOTEL

80 Wythe Avenue
(at N 11th St)
Williamsburg ⑨
+1 718 460 8000
www.wythehotel.com

Outside The Ides Bar on the 6th floor of the hotel is a wrap-around deck, allowing a lookout in four directions. More of a vista than a nestled-in view, it has a true calming effect, even though it's not that high. Watching the sun go down is popular here, so plan to go early.

285 THE VIEW

AT: NEW YORK MARRIOTT
MARQUIS HOTEL
1535 Broadway
(at W 45th St)
Midtown ⑥
+1 212 704 8900
www.theviewnyc.com

Let's face it: you're going to end up on Times Square some time during your stay in New York, so you might as well make a point to visit NYC's only revolving restaurant and lounge. Take the high-tech elevators up to the 47th and 48th floors and enjoy one 360° view rotation per hour – eat slowly.

282 ONE WORLD TRADE CENTER

5 *incredible*
PLACES OF WORSHIP

---

286 ELDRIDGE STREET SYNAGOGUE

12 Eldridge St
(betw Canal and
Division St)
Lower East Side ③
+1 212 219 0302
www.eldridgestreet.org

East European immigrants built this synagogue in 1887, one of the first in the US. Jewish numerology can be spotted: 12 rondels for the 12 tribes of Israel, 5 arches representing Books of Moses, and 4 wooden doors for the 4 matriarchs. Important Jewish families once frequented this beautiful space with soaring 70-foot ceilings and stained glass. Now a museum.

287 RIVERSIDE CHURCH

490 Riverside Drive
(at W 120th St)
Harlem ⑧
+1 212 870 6700
www.trcnyc.org

This church is famed for its Neo-Gothic architecture but even more so for its place in the fight for social justice. Martin Luther King Jr. spoke here against the Vietnam War. Cesar Chavez and Nelson Mandela visited it, as well as theological 'superstar' Reinhold Niebuhr. Boasts the largest *carillon* (bell tower).

288 ST MARK'S CHURCH-IN-THE-BOWERY

131 East 10th St
(at 2nd Ave)
East Village ④
+1 212 674 6377
www.stmarksbowery.org

The oldest site of continuous worship in Manhattan is still a progressive force honoring diversity and civil rights. Andy Warhol screened his early movies here. The Poetry Project, which many famous poets have read at, including Allen Ginsberg and Patti Smith, is still active today. Ongoing events include mindful meditation and discussions.

289 CATHEDRAL CHURCH OF ST JOHN THE DIVINE

1047 Amsterdam Avenue
(at W 112th St)
Morningside Heights ⑧
+1 212 316 7540
www.stjohndivine.org

World's largest cathedral, built by Freemasons, is a mecca of hidden symbolism carved into columns and sculpture, including references to its namesake, who had a vision of the end of the world. Annual rituals include The Blessing of the Animals, Procession of the Ghouls, The Blessing of the Bicycles, and a Winter Solstice Celebration.

290 CHURCH OF THE TRANSFIGURATION
"LITTLE CHURCH AROUND THE CORNER"

1 East 29th St (betw
5th and Madison Ave)
Midtown ⑥
+1 212 684 6770
www.littlechurch.org

Founded in 1848 to embrace all races, classes and sexual orientations, this early English Neo-Gothic style features a quaint English-style garden in front. Also known as the 'wedding church'. The complex includes eclectic side chapels and a 14th-century stained glass window. Free concerts in the main church.

VIEW FROM BROOKLYN BRIDGE PARK

75 PLACES TO DISCOVER NEW YORK

5 monuments to
GREAT MEN *and* WOMEN

291 **WASHINGTON SQUARE ARCH**
Washington Square Park (end of 5th Ave)
Greenwich Village ④

Sitting at the bottom of 5th Avenue, framing the fountain in Washington Square Park, this arch houses statues of George Washington. It was designed by Stanford White, who was inspired by Roman architecture and the Arc de Triomphe in Paris.

292 **MARQUIS DE LAFAYETTE**
Park Avenue South (at E 16th St and east end of Union Square)
Union Square ⑤

This French nobleman came to the aid of the colonies in their fight against the British during the Revolutionary War. The statue was designed by Frédéric-Auguste Bartholdi (who also designed the Statue of Liberty) and is a token of appreciation from the French government for aid provided during the Franco-Prussian War.

293 **ABRAHAM LINCOLN**
Union Square Park (north end of Park, at E 16th St)
Union Square ⑤

Cast in 1870, this larger-than-life bronze of Honest Abe looks south over the green quadrant of Union Square and the equestrian George Washington on the square's south end, both by sculptor Henry Kirke Brown. Controversy erupted when the statue was unveiled, due to the fact that Lincoln wore a toga over his suit.

294 FIORELLO LA GUARDIA

LaGuardia Place
(at Bleecker St)
Greenwich Village ④
www.nycgovparks.org

Upbeat statue of the 99th mayor of New York City, who served for three terms from 1934 to 1945. The famous New Deal Democrat was successful in linking national money with local needs. He was born in Greenwich Village, and was only 5,2 feet tall (1,57 meters) – hence his nickname, the 'Little Flower' (*fiorello* in Italian).

295 HARRIET TUBMAN

Memorial Plaza
West 122nd St,
St Nicholas Ave and
Frederick Douglass Blvd
Harlem ⑧
www.nycgovparks.org

Renowned American abolitionist. Born a slave, she escaped and helped numerous other slaves escape the South through the use of the so-called 'underground railroad'. Her dress depicts faces of slaves and some of the items they might have carried. Along the base are tiles that mimic quilt patterns with folk traditions.

291 WASHINGTON SQUARE ARCH

The 5 most impressive
MEMORIALS

296 **NATIONAL SEPTEMBER 11 MEMORIAL & MUSEUM**
AKA THE 9/11 MEMORIAL
180 Greenwich St (betw Cortlandt and Fulton St)
Financial District ①
+1 212 266 5211
www.911memorial.org

Two peaceful, identical pools with endless waterfalls flowing into them sit below walls inscribed with the names of the almost 3000 victims of that fateful day in 2001. The pools take up the same footprint as the original Twin Towers. This park-like memorial also has a museum with 9/11 artifacts.

297 **IRISH HUNGER MEMORIAL**
North End Ave and Vesey St
Battery Park City ①
+1 212 267 9799
www.bpcparks.org

Overlooking the Hudson river, an elevated grassy hill represents the Ireland so many immigrants left behind to build a future in New York, as a result of the Great Irish Famine (1845-1852). The hill contains stones from each of Ireland's 32 counties. Tip: grab a coffee in the small bar on the corner.

298 **GRANT'S TOMB**
Riverside Drive (at W 122nd St)
Harlem ⑧
+1 212 666 1640
www.nps.gov

The largest mausoleum in North America is that of Union Army general Ulysses S. Grant, who successfully defeated the Confederacy during the Civil War and went on to become the 18th president. Grant insisted on this location so his wife could be buried by his side.

299 AFRICAN BURIAL GROUND MEMORIAL

AT: TED WEISS FEDERAL
BUILDING
**290 Broadway (betw
Duane and Reade St)
Financial District** ⓘ
+1 212 637 2019
www.nps.gov/afbg

This recently discovered burial site contains the remains of 15.000 both free and enslaved Africans who lived in Manhattan from the late 1600s until 1794. The outdoor memorial was designed by Rodney Leon, and sits next to an exhibition space detailing the African contribution to the building of early New York City.

300 MUSEUM OF JEWISH HERITAGE

A LIVING MEMORIAL
TO THE HOLOCAUST
**36 Battery Place (inside
Battery Park near 1st Pl)
Battery Park City** ⓘ
+1 646 437 4202
www.mjhnyc.org

On the edge of the Hudson River lies a symbolic six-sided building with a pyramid roof, alluding to the 6 points of the Jewish star and the six million Jews who died during the Holocaust. Inside, a permanent exhibition utilizes personal accounts and artifacts of survivors. Check the calendar for other special exhibitions.

296 9/11 MEMORIAL

5

HISTORIC HOUSES

that fire the imagination

---

301 **MORRIS-JUMEL MANSION**
AT: ROGER MORRIS PARK
65 Jumel Terrace (betw
W 160th and 162nd St)
Washington Heights ⑧
+1 212 923 8008
www.morrisjumel.org

Manhattan's oldest house has had many illustrious dwellers. Built in 1765 as a country estate it also served as HQ for George Washington, was the home of Aaron Burr, and the outrageous and illegitimate daughter of a Rhode Island prostitute Eliza Bowen Jumel who became mistress of the house. Tour the house itself and current exhibition.

302 **HENRY CLAY FRICK HOUSE**
1 East 70th St
(at 5th Ave)
Upper East Side ⑦
+1 212 288 0700
www.frick.org

This Beaux Arts mansion was built in the 1910s for industrialist Henry Clay Frick, at a staggering cost of 5 million dollars. Using his steel fortune, Frick became a prominent collector of old masters such as Rembrandt, El Greco and Vermeer. At his death, he willed the house to be a public museum.

302 HENRY CLAY FRICK HOUSE

303 THEODORE ROOSEVELT BIRTHPLACE

28 East 20th St (betw Park Ave and Broadway)
Flatiron ⑤
+1 212 260 1616
www.nps.gov/thrb

The 26th president of the United States was born in a quaint townhouse. This museum is a replica of the original house rebuilt in 1919 and showcases many interesting objects from his time, like his Rough Rider uniform, his favorite chair, and an eyeglass case with bullet hole from an assassination attempt.

304 DYCKMAN FARMHOUSE MUSEUM

4881 Broadway
(at W 204th St)
Inwood ⑧
+1 212 304 9422
www.dyckman
farmhouse.org

The oldest surviving farmhouse on the island of Manhattan is a throw-back to the city's agrarian past. Built in Dutch colonial style around 1780 by William Dyckman, his family farmed the land well into the 19th century. Artifacts include family objects and archaeological objects from surrounding grounds, like cannon balls from the American Revolution.

305 THE MORGAN LIBRARY & MUSEUM

225 Madison Avenue
(at E 36th St)
Midtown ⑥
+1 212 685 0008
www.themorgan.org

Originally built to house the library of John Pierpont Morgan, financier and banker extraordinaire, presently a museum that holds his art collection – among other treasures. Peter Paul Rubens' drawings and the manuscript of Mozart's Haffner symphony are here. Architect Renzo Piano added a controversial, modern entrance to the library in 2006, his first project in New York.

5 *public library*
READING ROOMS

---

306 **ROSE MAIN READING ROOM**
AT: NEW YORK PUBLIC LIBRARY
476 Fifth Avenue
(at E 42nd St)
Midtown ⑥
+1 917 275 6975
www.nypl.org

This cathedral-like reading room is a true treasure, on par with the library Sainte-Geneviève in Paris. Newly restored to the tune of 12 million dollars, the impressive plaster ceiling – decorated with paintings of the sky, and gilded rosettes – has been reborn. The century-old Beaux-Arts room is 2 city blocks long, with 42 communal tables, and 52 ft ceilings.

307 **BROOKLYN PUBLIC LIBRARY**
FOR NEW YORKERS: CENTRAL LIBRARY
10 Grand Army Plaza
(at Flatbush Ave and Eastern Parkway)
Prospect Heights, Brooklyn ⑪
+1 718 230 2100
www.bklynlibrary.org

On the edge of Prospect Park sits a majestic, curved, Art Deco building highlighted by a jaw-dropping 50 ft entryway decked by 2 massive walls adorned with stylized gold-leaf figures. Fifteen bronze panels here celebrate icons of American literature – Edgar Allen Poe's *The Raven*, Mark Twain's *Tom Sawyer* and a whale for Herman Melville's *Moby Dick*.

308 THE EXPLORERS CLUB

46 East 70th St (betw
Park and Madison Ave)
Upper East Side ⑦
+1 212 628 8383
www.explorers.org

To gain access to this library you have to
make an appointment with this private
club's curator Lacey Flint, but the beauty
of what you'll find is more than worth
that small effort. You'll be impressed by
the 5000-volume map collection, and
Thor Heyerdahl's Kon-Tiki globe. The
1910 Jacobean mansion is filled with an
assortment of taxidermy and other global
travel souvenirs.

309 THE NEW YORK SOCIETY LIBRARY

53 East 79th St (betw
Madison and Park Ave)
Upper East Side ⑦
+1 212 288 6900
www.nysoclib.org

This five-story Italianate townhouse
houses the oldest library in the city full
of rare and exquisite books, founded
in 1754. It functioned as the Library of
Congress during New York's brief reign
as America's capitol. It it supported by its
members, but the first floor reading room
and exhibits are open to all.

310 THE GENERAL SOCIETY OF MECHANICS AND TRADESMEN LIBRARY

20 West 44th St
(betw 5th and 6th Ave)
Midtown ⑥
+1 212 840 1840
www.generalsociety.org

Contains more than 100.000 volumes
including books on various trades –
carpenters, blacksmiths, plumbers – that
have made up its membership. The main
reading room's magnificent space is
highlighted by an enormous copper-and-
wrought-iron skylight, and three stories
of balconies surrounding it, one of which
holds its collection of clever locks, one
dating back to Egypt BC.

5 city PARKS
to revel in

---

311 **THE HIGH LINE**
from Gansevoort and
Washington St to
W 34th St & 12th Ave
Multiple entrances
along 10th Ave
Chelsea ⑤
www.thehighline.org

A disused rail line from the 1930s has been transformed into a 1,5-mile-long landscaped wonderland, perched 30 ft above the street. An exciting new breed of modern building has taken over the area too – the HL 23, the crooked building on 23rd and the IAC Building, the frosted, amorphous giant between 18th and 19th Streets. Start your walk at the Whitney Museum.

312 **PROSPECT PARK**
Park Slope, Brooklyn ⑪
www.prospectpark.org

Olmsted and Vaux not only famously designed Central Park but also had a hand in the layout of this flagship Brooklyn park. It's the neighborhood's central hangout, much less manicured than its Manhattan cousin, with room for barbecues and impromptu soccer games. Walk or run on the looped trail and bridle path of roughly 4 continuous miles.

311 THE HIGH LINE

311 WHITNEY MUSEUM NEAR THE HIGH LINE

314 BATTERY PARK

313 INWOOD HILL PARK

Dyckman St
(at Payson Ave)
Inwood ⑧
www.nycgovparks.org

At the northwestern tip of Manhattan is 196 acres overlooking the Bronx, where you can also see two bridges spanning the East River, and a serene section of the Hudson. The natural forest, valleys and ridges hold remnants of the ancient and even prehistoric New York when the Lenape Native American tribes used the caves as dwellings.

314 BATTERY PARK

On the Hudson
(betw Battery Pl
and South St)
Battery Park City ①
www.nycgovparks.org

Battery Park is a beautifully landscaped 25-acre park that sits all the way downtown, right on the Hudson. It's where you'll get a view of the Statue of Liberty, pass a few museums and memorials. Choose to end your walk and watch the sun go down on Pier A, which was once a government building, now a fabulous blocks-long restaurant.

315 GREENWOOD CEMETERY

500 25th St
(at 5th Ave)
Brooklyn ⑪
+1 718 768 7300
www.green-wood.com

Founded in 1838 as one of the first rural cemeteries in America. Their 478 acres are donned with beautiful statuary and mausoleums, and a stunning entry gate. Check the calendar for events, like the annual tour of the catacombs. Famous folks buried here: artist Jean-Michel Basquiat, Leonard Bernstein, Frank Morgan – the wiz of *The Wizard of Oz*.

5

CENTRAL PARK

attractions

---

from Central Park West to Fifth Avenue
Central Park N to W 59th St
Central Park ⑦
+1 212 310 6600
www.centralparknyc.org

316 CONSERVATORY GARDEN
Betw 5th Ave and
E 105th St

A less traveled, more formal part of the park. Its 6 acres hold a special assortment of English, French and Italian flowers and is set up as a quiet zone, creating one of the more calm spots in Manhattan. Enter through the wrought iron Vanderbilt Gate, once the entry to a Vanderbilt estate before it was donated to the city.

317 MALL AND LITERARY WALK
On the east side of
the park, from E 67th
to 69th St

This grand promenade is the only straight path in Central Park, framed by beautiful American elm trees. Start at Center Drive, stroll past the Naumburg Bandshell to the Bethesda Terrace. At the southern end of the mall you can admire some sculptures. You may remember seeing the promenade in the movies *Kramer vs. Kramer* and *Maid in Manhattan*.

318 LAMP POST GPS

Lost? Use lamp posts to pinpoint where you are in the park. A small placard with four numbers is attached to each lamp post. The first two numbers represent the street, the second two numbers indicate if you are on the east or west side – even is east, odd is west.

319 NORTH WOODS

West side to mid park from W 101st to 110th St

The biggest of the three woodlands in the upper part of the park was designed to have a natural, wild look, with streams and archways leading to the peaceful Ravine at its heart. Walk through Loch's Tunnel, along the waterfalls (where you can spot turtles sunbathing) and feel far away from Manhattan.

320 STRAWBERRY FIELDS

West side of the park, betw W 71st and 74th St

A mandatory stop for those looking to connect with that songwriter from Liverpool, whose life was taken in front of his home at The Dakota building, around the corner. It's touristy, but maintains a somber, peaceful and respectful tone with The Garden of Peace, and the 'Imagine' mosaic built with funds donated by Yoko Ono.

5 *great neighborhood*
WALKS

---

321 **TRIBECA**

Immerse yourself in NYC's oldest neighborhood. See the earliest examples of decorative cast-iron buildings: Cast Iron House, 67 Franklin St; Obsidian House, 93 Reade St; 131 Duane St. The charming Hook & Ladder 8 firehouse from *Ghostbusters* at 14 N Moore St, and the row houses, on Harrison and Washington St.

322 **UPPER EAST SIDE**

After you hit one of the museums up on Museum Mile, take a stroll down Lexington Ave between 83rd St down to 69th St to soak up a slew of charming and independently owned coffee shops, boutiques, and old-times luncheonettes. Start at the Lexington Candy Shop, 1226 Lexington on the corner of 83rd St.

323 UPPER WEST SIDE

The UWS is known for its pretty tree-lined streets lined with characteristic townhouses — snake up and down the blocks from 69th to 76th, from Central Park West to Columbus. The Ansonia Hotel, a castle-like behemoth takes up an entire block on Broadway between 73rd and 74th Streets. Near the Museum of Natural History, NY Historical Society, The Dakota.

324 WEST VILLAGE

Bedford Street from Christopher to Houston is the fastest way to walk through the Village to Soho. On the way: narrowest house 75½ Bedford St; oldest house 77 Bedford St; some think the house on the corner of Grove and Bedford Streets (17 Grove) is the oldest; 102 Bedford St was renovated by an amateur architect in an odd style.

325 BROOKLYN BRIDGE PARK/DUMBO

Carousel at the end of Old Dock St

www.janescarousel.com

You can feel New York's past lingering in the streets, but also its future, thanks to the creative enterprises that have moved in. Must dos: take a picture on the corner of Water/Washington with Brooklyn Bridge looming; go for a ride on a beautifully-restored 1922 carousel, housed in a glass pavilion designed by Jean Nouvel.

325 BROOKLYN BRIDGE PARK

5 historic places in
BROOKLYN HEIGHTS

---

326 WOODEN HOUSES

along Middagh St
Brooklyn Heights ⑩

Wooden housing was outlawed in Brooklyn Heights in 1852 but some original wooden houses have remained along picturesque Middagh Street, namely numbers 31 and 24, on the corner of Willow Street. Truman Capote lived at 70 Willow St, by the way, and is known to have said: "I live in Brooklyn. By choice."

327 BROOKLYN HISTORICAL SOCIETY

128 Pierrepont St
(at Clinton St)
Brooklyn Heights ⑩
+1 718 222 4111
www.brooklynhistory.org

This museum aims to keep Brooklyn's 400-year history alive. It's housed in a beautiful red brick Romanesque Revival building from 1878 with arched windows and terra cotta detailing, including busts depicting the famous — Benjamin Franklin, Shakespeare, Beethoven, and Michelangelo. The interior houses a library with elegantly carved wooden bookcases and a dramatic mezzanine where many parties are held.

328 CHASE BANK BUILDING

177 Montague St
(at Clinton St)
Brooklyn Heights ⑩

This Italian Renaissance style building was built between 1914 and 1916 as a bank, and remarkably is still in use as a bank today. Take in the grandeur of the hall on the ground floor, with chandeliers hanging from the coffered ceiling, and the row of teller windows. The only signs of modernity are the ATMs that look totally out of place here.

329 SUPREME COURT BUILDING APPELLATE DIVISION

45 Monroe Place
(at Pierrepont St)
Brooklyn Heights ⑩
+1 718 875 1300

This stately Classical Revival courthouse was built between 1936 and 1938, in the style that flourished in the era of the Depression. It sits on the cusp of a residential neighborhood made up of mansions. Inside you can admire a two-story courtroom with a gold-leafed coffered ceiling.

330 BROOKLYN HEIGHTS PROMENADE

Betw Remsen and
Middagh St
Brooklyn Heights ⑩
www.nyharborparks.org

This 1800-ft (or 0,5-kilometer) walkway is also known as the Esplanade, and runs along the western edge of Brooklyn Heights. It's famous for its views of Lower Manhattan across the East River. Near Cranberry Street take the Squibb Park Bridge which meanders over the Brooklyn-Queens Expressway and connects to pier 1 of Brooklyn Bridge Park.

5 must-see
SPORTS

---

331 BASEBALL: THE YANKEES
YANKEE STADIUM
1 East 161st St (betw
River and Jerome Ave)
The Bronx
+1 718 293 4300
www.newyork.yankees.
mlb.com

The pin-striped Yankees are still the gold standard of NY baseball, whose players earn the big salaries, and have many championships under their belts. Watch them play in their newish 2,3 billion dollar stadium (most expensive one ever built). They get food from some of NYC's best restaurants, like Parm, Lobel's of New York, and Brother Jimmy's BBQ.

332 US OPEN
USTA BILLIE JEAN KING
NATIONAL TENNIS CENTER
ARTHUR ASHE STADIUM
Flushing Meadows
Corona Park
124-02 Roosevelt Avenue
(betw 60th and 61st St)
Queens
+1 718 760 6363
www.usopen.org

One of NYC's most sophisticated sporting events where professional tennis meets a see-and-be-seen enclave. Plenty of celebs and VIPs head to Queens each year at the end of August to watch the best in tennis compete. The matches go on for 12 days leading up to the exciting final showdowns. Tickets on sale in mid-June.

333 BASEBALL: THE METS
CITI FIELD
120-01 Roosevelt Avenue
(at Main St)
Queens
+1 718 507 8499
www.newyork.mets.
mlb.com

New York's # 2 baseball team probably has its most die-hard fans. The team has recently been playing very well – better than the Yankees. Shake Shack burgers can be had here, as well as celebrity-chef David Chang's chicken sandwiches. Once a year during the Subway Series, the Yankees and Mets play each other, to much NYC fanfare.

334 NY GIANTS
METLIFE STADIUM
1 MetLife Stadium Dr
East Rutherford, NJ
+1 201 935 8222
www.giants.com

The Giants are one of NY's football (American style) teams, whose stadium is in New Jersey. Tailgating is part of the fun, where fans gather in the parking lot with BBQs, and tons of food and drinks. Season tickets are the norm, but it's possible to purchase tickets to a single game on the website, sold individually by the ticket holders.

335 NYC MARATHON
www.tcsnycmarathon.org

Every first Sunday of November parts of New York become sectioned off for the marathon, one of the most prestigious in the world with over 50.000 runners, winding its way through all five boroughs. Cheering from sidelines happens all along the 26-mile route, with fans holding signs, playing *Eye of the Tiger*, and giving high fives to the runners.

5 ways to
SIGHTSEE
via public transport

---

336 **STATEN ISLAND FERRY**
Whitehall Terminal
Financial District ①
www.siferry.com

Instead of paying for a tour to float by the Statue of Liberty, hop on the Staten Island Ferry, whose 5-mile journey takes you through the New York harbor between the tip of Manhattan to Staten Island. The ferry operates 24/7 and is free. Staten Island side is currently being developed to house a mall and towering ferris wheel.

337 **IKEA EXPRESS FERRY**
Wall St – Pier 11
Financial District ①
+1 212 742 1969
www.nywatertaxi.com/ikea

Off a slip near the South Street Seaport, catch a ferry that takes you to the Ikea dock in Red Hook, Brooklyn. The 20-minute trip offers nice views of downtown. To explore Red Hook itself, take Beard St and walk 3 blocks to Van Brunt Street's many cool restaurants, including Fort Defiance. Free on the weekends.

338 **CROSS BRIDGES VIA THE SUBWAY**

Instead of going through a tunnel, opt to connect from Manhattan to Brooklyn via a bridge. To cross over the Manhattan Bridge take the B, D, N, or Q trains, where you'll end up in Fort Greene and beyond. For the Williamsburg Bridge get on the J, M, or Z trains to stops in Williamsburg and beyond.

339 M5 BUS DOWN FIFTH AVENUE

Upper East Side ⑦ +
Midtown ⑥
www.bustime.mta.info

Fifth Avenue is still NYC's main upscale thoroughfare and you can get a glimpse of its shine as you ride from 59th to 42nd street. Lined with the crème de la crème: designer stores, posh hotels, Rockefeller Center. Due to traffic, you'll be moving slowly, so you can take it all in. Even more dramatic at night especially during the holidays.

340 ROOSEVELT ISLAND TRAMWAY

East 59th St
(at 2nd Ave)
Upper East Side ⑦
+1 212 832 4555
www.rioc.ny.gov

Use your MTA subway card and take the aerial tramway that spans the East River and connects Manhattan with Roosevelt Island – at dramatic heights. You'll experience soaring views, and perhaps a bit of acrophobia, in the 5 minutes that it takes to career you across. When you get there, take a stroll along the river.

336 STATEN ISLAND FERRY

The 5 best ways to
M I N G L E *with New Yorkers*

---

341 PLAY CHESS IN THE PARK

Match wits with those who have made this a daily sport. It's usually 5 dollars a game, played in a most speedy way. Look for guys in the SW corner of Washington Square Park (some cheating and trash talk!), the west side of Union Square Park, and Central Park's Chess and Checkers House off 65th Street.

342 DINE AT THE BAR INSTEAD OF AT A TABLE

Solo and duo diners, this is your chance to engage in conversation, and dine at those restaurants where it's nearly impossible to get a reservation. Most restaurants will allow you to set up shop at the bar, but some places encourage it, like: Cosme, Union Square Cafe, Acme, Casa Mono.

343 ANNUAL FEAST OF SAN GENNARO

Along Mulberry St
Little Italy ③
www.sangenarro.org

This 11-day event is something that every New Yorker has done at least once in their life. Mulberry Street turns into a carnival of sorts with musical acts, games, and authentic Italian eats. A religious procession honors the saint rumored to have survived the flames of a fiery furnace.

344 **CENTRAL PARK DANCE SKATERS ASSOCIATION**
Central Park ⑦
cpdsa.org

Flock to the Bandshell in Central Park to watch free-spirited dancing/skating. There are terrifically skilled performers, some who have been coming since the 70s when this phenomenon started. Weekends April-October. Inspired? Head to Pier 2 Roller Rink in Brooklyn Bridge Park, rent skates and strut your stuff.

345 **WATCH A PARADE**

NYC hosts over 30 parades a year, bringing out the population to view. There are the well-known spectacles, like the Macy's Thanksgiving Parade, but dig deeper to find smaller, fun processions like the colorful Lunar New Year in Chinatown, the Easter Parade where everyone dons their finest bonnets, and the Gay Pride where anyone can march.

345 WATCH A PARADE

5 ways to enjoy
N Y C *from the water*

---

346 FREE KAYAKING FROM PIER 26
THE NEW YORK CITY DOWNTOWN BOATHOUSE

Hubert St
(at the Hudson River)
TriBeCa ③
www.downtownboat-
house.org

Get up close and personal on the Hudson in 20-minute spurts. NYCDB also holds free classes that will help to perfect your paddling technique, and how not to panic if you capsize. Longer guided trips are available on a first come, first serve basis. (There are six other spots to launch from around NYC.)

347 QUIET CLUBBING PARTY CRUISE
CIRCLE LINE PIER 83

West 42nd St
(at the Hudson River)
Midtown West ⑥
+1 212 563 3200
www.circleline42.com

A new trend for dance pop-ups involves wearing headphones and tuning into one of 3 DJs. Kind of eerie to watch, but so much fun to participate. They have taken to the water on a party boat with a massive outdoor dance floor on roof, so you can shake it up while cruising under the Brooklyn Bridge.

348 INTREPID SEA, AIR & SPACE MUSEUM

PIER 86
West 46th St
(at 12th Ave)
Midtown West ⑥
+1 212 245 0072
www.intrepidmuseum.org

Like being transported back to the 1940s. There's plenty to see on this aircraft carrier, including the Concorde, historic military aircraft, the space shuttle Enterprise and a look inside a submarine – plus exhibits in the military genre. Note, during hot weather the deck can get pretty hot, or conversely, windy and cold.

349 BATEAUX NEW YORK DINNER CRUISES

PIER 62
West 23rd St
Chelsea ⑤
+1 866 817 3463
www.bateaux
newyork.com

For an upscale dining experience while riding the waves, head off the pier in Chelsea for three hours of fun. It's possible to reserve tables next to the windows so you can focus on the towering skyscrapers – this boat has a glass roof, so you can see from almost any spot. Dress up and treat yourself.

350 WALK OVER THE BROOKLYN OR WILLIAMSBURG BRIDGE

Brooklyn Bridge: From the Manhattan side enter at Centre and Chambers. From the Brooklyn side enter at Tillary and Brooklyn Bridge Boulevard or at the NE side of Cadman Plaza. Less congested is Williamsburg Bridge: From the Manhattan side pedestrians and cyclists enter at Clinton and Delancey. From Williamsburg pedestrians enter at Berry Street between 5th and 6th Streets and cyclists ride up at Washington Plaza.

The 5 best ways to get
PHYSICAL

---

351 WHERE TO GO FOR A RUN

Thanks to NY governor Mario Cuomo, there's a running path along the Hudson River from the tip of Manhattan to the Bronx with bathrooms and kiosks along the way. In Central Park, the full loop is about 6 miles; the 1,58-mile track along the Jacqueline Onassis Reservoir is known as the 'Stephanie and Fred Shurman Running Track' in recognition of a donation for the renovation – and is the path that Dustin Hoffman runs in the movie *Marathon Man*.

352 WEST 4TH STREET BASKETBALL COURTS

Corner of West 4th St
and 6th Avenue
Greenwich Village ④

A legendary gathering spot for exemplary players and onlookers. On this smaller than regulation-size court, also known as 'The Cage', tough physical play is the norm. It's fast and hard, with a lot of yelling and unwanted coaching from the courtside. Exhilarating to watch the talented players, some of whom become NBA stars, like Knick Anthony Mason.

353 CLASSPASS

www.classpass.com

Buy a monthly pass and find innovative and in-demand fitness classes all around NYC's boutique gym studios for less. They offer 5 classes for 19 dollars in their 1-month base trial. Search and book yoga classes, spin, barre, pilates, dance, martial arts, boxing and more – it's a great way to learn about different fitness genres.

354 CITIBIKE

+1 855 245 3311
www.citibikenyc.com

Set up in areas all throughout Manhattan, Brooklyn, and Queens, Citibike allows you to rent a bike, and drop at any of their locations. The trick is, you must return the bike within 30 minutes – or rack up fees, 4 dollars for each additional 15 minutes, so plan ahead. For 12 dollars you can buy a day-pass with unlimited 30 minute rides.

355 SAL ANTHONY'S MOVEMENT SALON

190 Third Avenue
(betw E 17th and 18th St)
Gramercy ⑤
+1 212 420 7242
www.movementsalon.com

It's all about innovation here – in a space once a German *Ratskeller* which still has the elaborate stained glass art on its high ceiling. Enjoy pilates machine classes, Gyrotonic, a pulley-system that stretches as you go, and A.I.M., Anthony's signature movement system involving hanging from 2 straps, to loosen all your muscles and cares. Best massage in the city for the price.

5 eras to witness **NYC** in **BOOKS** and **MOVIES**

356 **HISTORY AND ORIGINS OF MANHATTAN**

Forever by Pete Hamill takes you through Manhattan's earliest days to the present, with an imaginative tale of a man who is graced with the ability to live forever; *Burr* by Gore Vidal paints a portrait of the early city and its political dramas; *Manahatta* by Eric Sanderson illustrates the city's wild, natural beginnings.

357 **50S, 60S, 70S DYNAMICS**

Just Kids, Patti Smith's memoir of her friendship with artist Robert Mapplethorpe, paints an accurate picture of Soho's artist beginnings and subculture of Manhattan; *Sleeping with Bad Boys* by Alice Denham, is an aspiring writer's tell-all of her trysts with the famous in the 1950s. Movies *Taxi Driver* and *Rosemary's Baby* capture the ultra gritty 60s and 70s city.

358 RE-LIVING THE 1980S-1990S

Desperately Seeking Susan, *American Psycho*, and *Do the Right Thing* are three films depicting NYC in the scene-changing eighties – pitching class and race and anti-establishment groups against each other. *Killing Williamsburg* by Bradley Spinelli captures the days of a 1990s gentrifying Williamsburg which is also going through an eerie suicide spree.

359 BACK TO THE 1800S

Hester Street, a movie that tells the story of a Jewish family who immigrated to the Lower East Side and how they ultimately assimilated; *Time And Again* is the classic time-travel tale by Jack Finney whose story takes place at The Dakota and on Gramercy Park – a mystery and moving love story.

360 THROUGH THE EYES OF WOODY ALLEN

Witness this artist's romance with the city. *Manhattan* is brilliant in its black-and-white cinematography, showing viewpoints and scenes from 1979. *Annie Hall*, out in 1977, highlights NYC vs LA attitudes. *Manhattan Murder Mystery* is a great slice of life focused on two couples who suspect their neighbor has murdered his wife, circa 1993.

5 things that
NEW YORKERS
just KNOW

---

361 **TAXI SAVVY**

No cabs in sight? The next best thing is Uber or Lyft, but to avoid costly surge pricing download the taxi apps. Arro and Curb work the same way, but with professional drivers in yellow cabs. Also good to know, when a taxi has its Off Duty sign lit, cabs can still pick you up if your destination is on their way home.

362 **PUBLIC RESTROOMS**

Public restrooms are few and far between. You might see some in parks, or have to stop and get something in a restaurant, but the fact is most hotel lobby's won't stop you from coming in. So act like you're staying there and take advantage. There's also NYrestroom.com that maps the city's options.

363 DRESS APPROPRIATELY

Walking is the best way to get around and really get to see all that's out there. So, bring your favorite, stylish pair of comfortable footwear that can work the scene from day to night. Smart casual outfits, athleisure, and a chill attitude can get you in almost anywhere. Black still reigns, but is waning.

364 RESTAURANT RULES

If you want to get into a hot restaurant it's best to plan ahead. Go online to OpenTable.com or Resy.com to check availability and reserve. Lots of restaurants are closed on Mondays, with busiest nights being Thursdays and Fridays. Summer weekends leave the city less populated, so perfect for getting that Saturday night table, especially 3-day weekends.

365 SAMPLE SALES AND POP-UPS

Find designer goods at 50-90% off. Check Chicmi.com, where they list sample sales and conveniently show others nearby – so you can really take advantage of the deals. Pop-Up stores fill empty retail space with racks of designer goods too. Go to 260samplesale.com to see who's selling. Bigger sales/shows have admission fees.

FRANK LLOYD WRIGHT ROOM

60 WAYS
TO ENJOY CULTURE

---

5 well-established
GALLERIES

---

366 DAVID ZWIRNER GALLERY
537 West 20th St
(betw 10th and 11th Ave)
Chelsea ⑤
+1 212 517 8677
www.davidzwirner.com

David Zwirner opened his first gallery in Soho in 1993. His latest in NYC is in a 30.000-sq-foot sleek building designed to accommodate large installations. The gallery is home to many highly regarded artists, like Jeff Koons, Yayoi Kusama, Luc Tuymans, Neo Rauch, and William Eggleston.

367 HAUSER & WIRTH
548 West 22nd St
(betw W 10th and 11th Ave)
Chelsea ⑤
+1 212 790 3900
www.hauserwirth.com

This internationally renowned and respected Swiss-owned gallery has moved its digs into temporary quarters in the former DIA space, while awaiting the construction of a brand-new space next door. The gallery represents established and emerging artists, including Mark Bradford, and Paul McCarthy and artist estates, like The Louise Bourgeois Studio.

368 GAGOSIAN GALLERY

976 Madison Avenue
(betw E 76th and
77th St)
Upper East Side ⑦
+1 212 744 2313
www.gagosian.com

Larry Gagosian is consistently listed in the top 10 of *ArtReview*'s Power 100, with 16 galleries around the world. In New York you can visit four of them, two uptown, and two in Chelsea. If you can't afford to buy the art, you might be able to pick up something cool from the shop.

369 BARBARA GLADSTONE

530 West 21st St
(betw 10th and 11th Ave)
Chelsea ⑤
+1 212 206 7606
www.gladstone
gallery.com

American art dealer and film producer Barbara Gladstone has been a gallery owner for more than 25 years and kept her finger on the pulse. Her vision is behind some of the most successful contemporary artists today, such as Matthew Barney. The stark minimalist cube of a building includes an exhibit space with 22-ft ceilings and enormous skylight.

370 BLUM & POE

19 East 66th St
(betw 5th and
Madison Ave)
Upper East Side ⑦
+1 212 249 2249
www.blumandpoe.com

The Los Angeles titan's New York outpost offers museum-quality contemporary art with their very particular spin, in a more intimate setting – on the top two floors of a townhouse. Chuck Close and Julian Schnabel are just two of the quite famous artists they represent, along with groundbreaking art from Asia.

5 *interesting*
AVANT-GARDE
GALLERIES

---

371 GAVIN BROWN'S ENTERPRISE
429 West 127th St
(betw Convent and
Amsterdam Ave)
Harlem ⑧
+1 212 627 5258
www.gavinbrown.biz

One of the coolest and most influential galleries in town for over 25 years. His newest incarnation occupies three floors of a former brewery in Harlem – whose inaugural exhibition featured work by Ed Atkins, a British artist known for his video art of disturbingly-real avatars blended with poetry.

372 BRIDGET DONAHUE GALLERY
99 Bowery, 2nd floor
(betw Hester and
Grand St)
Lower East Side ③
+1 646 896 1386
www.bridgetdonahue.nyc

This is where artists go when they want to know what's happening. Thanks to Bridget Donahue's focus on underrated artists, her gallery is considered a hub of the new generation and a bright beacon on the Lower East Side. She also has a hand in the fantastic gallery Cleopatra's in Brooklyn.

373 RAMIKEN CRUCIBLE

389 Grand St (betw
Essex and Clinton St)
Lower East Side ③
+1 917 328 4656
www.ramiken
crucible.com

This bad-ass gallery is the brainchild
of musician and artist Mike Egan, who
was described by the New York Times
as 'Marcel Duchamp's non-existent
mischievous little brother'. He regularly
hosts music performances in this raw
space, whose art is the most cutting-edge,
with artists like Lucas Blalock.

374 JTT

191 Chrystie St
(betw Stanton and
Rivington St)
Lower East Side ③
+1 212 574 8152
www.jttnyc.com

This longtime LES gallery district mainstay
has tripled in size at its new 1500-sq-ft
space, one floor up, around the corner
from the New Museum. The gallery has
absolutely the best artists list, including
idiosyncratic painting and assemblages
by Borna Sammak and sculptural
installations by Anna-Sophie Berger.

375 AMERICAN MEDIUM

515 West 20th St
(betw 10th and 11th Ave)
Chelsea ⑤
+1 201 396 7642
www.american
medium.net

What started in the edgy neighborhood
of Bed-Stuy Brooklyn has replanted and
expanded itself in Chelsea. Three young
visionaries specialize in discovering
new digital-based artists. The new space
allows for more performance, and
though set amongst the elite galleries
in the neighborhood, has retained
a raw sensibility.

5 places where you can enjoy
ART FOR FREE

376 CHRISTIE'S
20 Rockefeller Plaza
(betw W 48th and
49th St)
Midtown ⑥
+1 212 636 2000
www.christies.com

This world renowned auction house is located right in the heart of the city. All objects up for auction appear on display – where you can view free of charge. Check the calendar to see what lots are on view, and you may just return home with a treasure.

377 SOTHEBY'S
1334 York Avenue
(at E 72nd St)
Upper East Side ⑦
+1 212 606 7000
www.sothebys.com

So much valuable art passes through Sotheby's that it's worth the trek to the East River – you never know what you might find. Head to the auction rooms on the second floor to marvel at this month's selection of fine and decorative art, jewelry, and collectibles.

378 PHILLIPS
450 Park Avenue
(betw E 56th and 57th St)
Midtown East ⑥
+1 212 940 1300
www.phillips.com

The place to buy and sell objects from the 20th and 21st centuries: original artwork by Andy Warhol, Banksy, and Keith Haring; furniture by Hans J. Wegner, Emile-Jacques Ruhlmann, or Le Corbusier; jewelry from Cartier and Van Cleef & Arpels; or photos by Man Ray, Edward Weston, Irving Penn, and Cindy Sherman.

379 MUSEUM'S FREE DAYS
All Over Town

Check websites for exact times: TUES: Brooklyn Botanic Garden; Cooper-Hewitt; Jewish Museum. WED: Bronx Museum of the Arts; Children's Museum of the Arts. THURS: New Museum of Contemporary Art. FRI: Asia Society; MoMA; The Morgan Library; The Neue Galerie. SAT: Brooklyn Botanic Garden; Brooklyn Museum; Studio Museum in Harlem.

380 ART IN THE PARKS
Madison Square Park
East 23rd-26th St, betw
Madison and 5th Ave
Flatiron ⑤
www.madisonsquare
park.org

Massive sculptures grace the lawns of Madison Square Park on an ongoing basis. Art works on view are presented by Madison Square Park Conservancy. While in the park, hit the line and enjoy a famous Shake Shack burger.

377 SOTHEBY'S

The 5 best
ART FAIRS

---

381 FRIEZE NEW YORK
Randall's Island Park
Queens
+1 212 463 7488
www.frieze.com

Every year in the beginning of May a giant tent on Randall's Island Park sets up on the East River. For two days, the world's leading contemporary art galleries arrive, representing over 1000 of today's most important artists. Arriving via ferry is the stylish way to go, or via bus from the Guggenheim.

382 TEFAF
AT: PARK AVENUE ARMORY
643 Park Avenue
(at E 66th St)
Upper East Side ⑦
+1 212 616 3930
www.tefaf.com

Maastricht's TEFAF fair landed in New York in 2016 and opened with a bang – a newly discovered Van Gogh. The spring edition (in early May) focuses on contemporary art and design. At the fall edition (end of October) dealers arrive with their best pieces of decorative art from Antiquity to 1920, with an opening night benefit.

383 THE ART SHOW

AT: PARK AVENUE ARMORY
643 Park Avenue
(at 67th St)
Upper East Side ⑦
+1 212 488 5550
www.artdealers.org

Organized by the Art Dealers Association of America (ADAA), this art show is considered to be the best one in New York, with presentations by 72 of America's leading art dealers, selling works from the 19th century to today. The show goes for 5 days in the beginning of March, opening with a gala preview.

384 THE ARMORY SHOW

PIERS 92 & 94
711 Twelfth Avenue
(at W 55th St)
Midtown West ⑥
+1 212 645 6440
www.thearmoryshow.com

The city's premier art fair for discovering 20th- and 21st-century pieces takes place every year for 4 days in the beginning of March on two long piers jutting into the Hudson. There are panel discussions, artist talks, book signings, and Focus – the section to encounter new artists and galleries.

385 AFFORDABLE ART FAIR NYC

AT: THE METROPOLITAN PAVILION
125 West 18th St
(betw 6th and 7th Ave)
Chelsea ⑤
+1 212 255 2003
www.affordable artfair.com

At the end of March, more than 70 exhibitors offer an array of original art selling from 100 to 10.000 dollars, with the majority under 5000 dollars, by established artists and rising stars. Check the schedule of artist performances, innovative talks and tours, and hands-on workshops also happening.

5 must-see areas of the
MET

Metropolitan Museum of Art
1000 Fifth Avenue (at E 82nd St)
Central Park ⑦
+1 212 535 7710
www.metmuseum.org

386 PANORAMIC VIEW OF THE PALACE AND GARDENS OF VERSAILLES

Gallery 735
Inside the American Wing

In the 1700s this was considered a form of sightseeing – rooms set up in a 360° setting which made it seem as if you were actually there. This view of Versailles by John Vanderlyn was painted in New York using the sketches that he had made at Versailles in 1814. The artist toured with his masterpiece and included a self-portrait, pointing (on the right of the Basin de Latone).

387 FRANK LLOYD WRIGHT ROOM

Gallery 745
Inside the American Wing

The spacious living room from one of Frank Lloyd Wright's grandest prairie houses is meticulously recreated to the very last detail. The house was owned by the Little family, a member wanting a smaller house on the land chose to sell it to the Met, who have honored the original intentions of the designer, including daylight coming in through the wall of windows.

388 SHADY LADIES TOUR
throughout the museum
www.shadyladiestours.com

Shady Ladies Tours points out the museum's artwork depicting courtesans, mistresses, and professional beauties throughout history – complete with their accompanying scandalous backstories, led by scholar and professor Andrew Lear, an expert on Greek and Roman erotic art. They also have a Gay Secrets of the Met and a Sexy Secrets of the Met Tours.

389 HENRY R. LUCE CENTER
mezzanine of
the American Wing

View those American fine art and decorative art objects that are not currently on display in the museum. Called 'visible art storage' this back room of the museum is open to all visitors. Meticulously arranged by material, form and chronology, the collection includes oil paintings, sculpture, furniture and woodwork, glass, ceramics, and metalwork.

390 THE ISLAMIC WING

Opened in 2011, this wing includes 15 galleries displaying treasures from across the Islamic world. Don't miss: the 14th-century prayer niche outfitted in an intricate mosaic of blue, white and turquoise tiles; rare, astonishingly beautiful carpets from the 1500s; the Damascus Room, a reconstruction of a room from a house in Syria in 1707.

The 5 most intimate
MUSEUMS

---

391 EL MUSEO DEL BARRIO
1230 Fifth Avenue
(at 104th St)
Upper East Side ⑦
+1 212 831 7272
www.elmuseo.org

The city's only museum dedicated to Puerto Rican, Caribbean and Latin American modern art, graphics, pre-Columbian, and devotional arts (like those of Orisha-worshippers). Exhibitions are complemented by film screenings, The Coqui Club for bilingual tots, plus literary and performing arts. Nighttime, attend fun events with DJs, live music, and pop-up installations.

392 TENEMENT MUSEUM
103 Orchard St
(at Delancey St)
Lower East Side ③
+1 877 975 3786
www.tenement.org

Take a guided tour and meet the residents (played by actors). This building, where more than 7000 immigrants passed through, was built in 1863. The house is staged to look exactly the way it did when the immigrants lived there. People are encouraged to share their own stories to preserve the history of NYC's early immigration.

393 THE NEW MUSEUM

235 Bowery
(betw Stanton and
Rivington St)
Lower East Side ③
+1 212 219 1222
www.newmuseum.org

The museum presents work of under-recognized and emerging international artists before they receive widespread attention – with works that are often considered out-of-the-ordinary. It is where gallery-owner Barbara Gladstone established the Stuart Regen Fund to support lecture series by leading international thinkers in the fields of art, architecture, design. The building itself, makes a cool statement on Bowery.

394 NEUE GALLERIE

1048 Fifth Avenue
(at E 86th St)
Upper East Side ⑦
+1 212 994 9493
www.neuegalerie.org

The place for turn-of-the-century German and Austrian art and design. There are stunning tabletop items by Josef Hoffman and others, drawings and paintings by Gustav Klimt, Oskar Kokoschka, and Egon Schiele – all tucked inside a Beaux-Arts mansion. An authentic, lovely Viennese cafe sits inside, which also hosts live European music of the 1890s-1930s on Thursday nights.

395 DONALD JUDD HOUSE

101 Spring St
(at Mercer St)
Soho ②
+1 212 219 2747
www.juddfoundation.org

The artist purchased this building in 1968 and turned it into his playground for creating. In homage, his home and studio have been made to look exactly the way they did in 1994 – leaving everything in place (200 pieces of art and furniture plus 1800 household items). Only groups of 8 at a time can tour, book in advance.

5 of the best places to see
DANCE

396 JOYCE THEATER
175 Eighth Avenue
(at W 19th St)
Chelsea ⑤
+1 212 242 0800
www.joyce.org

The Joyce's programming covers many different styles of contemporary and cutting-edge dance like jazz-inspired tap-dancing and flamenco along with traditional ballet – and the avant-garde Ballet Hispanico. Reserve a spot at intermission to enjoy your glass of bubbly at a table and rub elbows with fellow dance enthusiasts.

397 THE KITCHEN
512 West 19th St
(betw 10th Ave
and West St)
Chelsea ⑤
+1 212 255 5793
www.thekitchen.org

For those seeking the truly outlandish and experimental. The Kitchen is one of NYC's oldest nonprofit spaces where artists like Laurie Anderson, Lucinda Childs, and Bill T. Jones have debuted. Shows feature experimental dance by innovative, boundary-pushing artists. The space also features music, theater, video, art, and talks.

398 SYMPHONY SPACE

**2537 Broadway
(at W 95th St)
Upper West Side ⑦
+1 212 864 5400
www.symphonyspace.org**

Symphony Space hosts music, dance, theater, film, and readings (known for Selected Shorts – where famous actors read engaging short stories). There are two performance spaces: the 800-seat Peter Jay Sharp Theatre, and the more intimate 170-seat Leonard Nimoy Thalia, named after two of their most illustrious patrons.

399 BROOKLYN ACADEMY OF MUSIC

**30 Lafayette Avenue
(betw St Felix St and
Ashland Pl)
Fort Greene, Brooklyn ⑩
+1 718 636 4100
www.bam.org**

To see an eclectic mix of dance, often described as energetic, frenetic, and dazzling interpretations of classics, head to BAM. They also feature film, theater, music, and operas performed by adventurous artists, some emerging and others known masters. This venue has three theaters, the Harvey Theater, Peter Jay Sharp Building, and the Fisher Building.

400 HOUSE OF YES

**2 Wyckoff Avenue
(at Jefferson St)
Bushwick, Brooklyn
www.houseofyes.org**

Opened in 2016, this colorful cube pushes the boundaries of entertainment. Shows include an attractive assortment of aerialists, magicians, dancers, and live bands. If dressing up is your thing, you will fit in with this crowd, who love to arrive in outlandish and creative outfits. Doors open early, with bar and DJ while you await the show.

5 intimate
THEATERS

---

401 59E59 THEATERS
59 East 59th St (betw
Park and Madison Ave)
Midtown East ⑥
+1 212 753 5959
www.59e59.org

A wonderful, small theater experience showcasing new work from around the world to premiere in NYC. Their four floors house three theaters running fun, innovative, and experimental works. Shows run for roughly a month, so there's always something new to see. The Brits Off Broadway series is a yearly festival that imports works from the UK.

402 LA MAMA EXPERIMENTAL THEATRE CLUB
66 East 4th St (betw
Bowery and 2nd Ave)
East Village ④
+1 212 352 3101
www.lamama.org

Ellen Stewart, a true supporter of the arts, founded La Mama in 1961. Since then a slew of playwrights (Sam Shepard) and celebs (Robert De Niro, Whoopi Goldberg, Bette Midler) have graced the space. Over 100 productions take place annually at their three theaters. Shows usually run for a few weeks, or can be a single performance.

403 MCKITTRICK HOTEL

530 West 27th St
(betw 10th and 11th Ave)
Chelsea ⑤
+1 866 811 4111
www.mckittrickhotel.com

A theater 'experience' which allows guests to walk through 5 floors of the fictitional McKittrick Hotel at their own pace. Actors perform a silent, modern adaptation of Macbeth, called *Sleep No More*, while guests don masks. Surprises are in store. Viewing solo is strongly encouraged to make the most of the night – follow the sounds of the music.

404 CHERRY LANE THEATRE

38 Commerce St
(betw Bedford Ave
and Hudson St)
West Village ④
+1 212 989 2020
www.cherrylane
theatre.org

On one of the most quaint curving streets in the West Village is an equally becoming theater. Long a home for non-traditional and experimental works, you can sit in comfort and witness theater in an intimate setting. Productions range from new works by emerging playwrights to classics from the icons of theater.

405 THEATRE 80 ST MARKS

80 St Marks Place
(betw 1st and 2nd Ave)
East Village ④
+1 212 388 0388
www.theatre80.
wordpress.com

Enter through an old tavern to experience this intimate theater with history – a pioneer in the downtown arts movement. Sidewalk out front still features footprints of visiting stars – including Gloria Swanson. Today, their shows range from traditional Shakespeare to avant-garde works from new authors.

The 5 best places to hear
JAZZ

---

406 ZINC BAR
82 West 3rd St
(betw Thompson and
Sullivan St)
Greenwich Village ④
+1 212 477 9462
www.zincbar.com

A cool subterranean jazz club, with an Art-Deco, red-velvety, Parisian vibe. It holds the spirit of the place when it was home to Thelonious Monk and Billie Holliday. Finger tap to African, Latin and Brazilian rhythms on the weekends. Thursdays feature the wild card sets.

407 SMALLS JAZZ CLUB
183 West 10th St
(betw 7 Ave S and
W 4th St)
Greenwich Village ④
+1 646 476 4346
www.smallslive.com

A destination spot for great jazz, the atmosphere is authentic, not slick; you'll feel like you're in an old-school New York jazz club of a bygone era. No reservations. To get a preview, become a member of SmallsLIVE to watch live streams, every show has been recorded since 2007.

408 BLUE NOTE JAZZ CLUB
131 West 3rd St
(betw MacDougal St
and 6th Ave)
Greenwich Village ④
+1 212 475 8592
www.bluenote.net

The spot to see the jazz's finest musicians, just look for the building with the grand piano-shaped awning. If you go to the Monday Night Series or the Late Night Groove Series you'll witness New York's up-and-coming jazz, soul, hip-hop, R&B and funk artists as well. Be prepared to stand in line.

409 BIRDLAND JAZZ CLUB

315 West 44th St
(betw 8th and 9th Ave)
Hell's Kitchen ⑥
+1 212 581 3080
www.birdlandjazz.com

More of a supper club than intimate venue, this space was built for world-class jazz — with great acoustics. Tune into the sounds of legendary musicians like Oscar Peterson, Diana Krall, Dave Brubeck, Tito Puente, along with big bands, while enjoying food with Cajun-influence. They host the Umbria Jazz Festival and the Django Reinhardt Festival.

410 GRAMERCY PARK HOTEL

2 Lexington Avenue
(betw E 21st and 22nd St)
Gramercy ⑤
+1 212 920 3300
www.gramercypark
hotel.com

Experience a nostalgic sampling of jazz standards and original songs by trumpeter Brian Newman at Rose Bar every Tuesday and Thursday night. AKA Lady Gaga's bandleader, Newman belts out tunes with personality and flair. The lush room in the hotel is set up with cushy couches and artwork from 20th-century masters.

408 BLUE NOTE JAZZ CLUB

The 5 best
CLUBS
for a night out

---

411 UPRIGHT CITIZENS BRIGADE THEATER

555 West 42nd St
(betw 10th and 11th Ave)
Hells Kitchen ⑥
+1 212 366 9176
hellskitchen.ucbtheatre.com

The improv and sketch comedy groups that perform here are some of the best in the city. Some stars of *Saturday Night Live* and writers for late-night talk shows like to show up at ASSSSCAT 3000 on Sunday nights. Other noteworthy teams include Death by Roo Roo (Saturdays) and the Stepfathers (Fridays).

412 COMEDY CELLAR

117 MacDougal St
(betw Minetta Lane
and W 3rd St)
Greenwich Village ④
+1 212 254 3480
www.comedycellar.com

This well-known comedy club was immortalized by comedian Louis C.K. in the opening credits of his TV show *Louie* and has hosted most of comedy's luminaries – who still often drop in impromptu. *The Nasty Show* on Wednesdays and Thursdays allows comics to spew out some of their more shocking material.

413 WEBSTER HALL

125 East 11th St
(betw 3rd and 4th Ave)
East Village ④
+1 212 353 1600
www.websterhall.com

The biggest and most prestigious nightclub and performance hall in New York City. Webster Hall has been around since 1886 and has seen everything from masquerade balls in the 20s to Mick Jagger and Metallica. Five different venues inside.

414 KNITTING FACTORY

**361 Metropolitan Avenue
(betw N 4th and 5th St)
Williamsburg ⑨
+1 347 529 6696
*bk.knittingfactory.com***

This nightclub moved from Soho to TriBeCa to Williamsburg bringing its eclectic music and entertainment program. The Main Venue where the performances take place has an open floor, and The Front Bar is where you can bide time before a show, or have a more intimate experience, like comedy on Sunday nights.

415 BOSSA NOVA CIVIC CLUB

**1271 Myrtle Avenue
(at Hart St)
Bushwick, Brooklyn
+1 718 443 1271
*www.bossanova
civicclub.com***

Under the elevated train is a club known for their sound system and DJ lineup focused on mostly underground house and techno. People come here to dance (especially on Monday nights), but in front there's a spot to lounge as well. No cover, dress code, and daily happy hour from 5 to 10 pm.

412 COMEDY CELLAR

The 5 best places to watch
FILMS

---

416 BRYANT PARK FILM FESTIVAL
Betw W 40th-42nd St and 5th-6th Avenue Midtown ⑥
+1 212 768 4242
www.bryantpark.org

Like a drive-in movie theater, but in the open air at Bryant Park, surrounded by office towers and the New York Public Library. The lawn opens at 5 pm, and gets filled quickly with people on blankets awaiting the show that starts at sunset. Tote some take-out and grab a spot early to mix and mingle.

417 METROGRAPH
7 Ludlow St (betw Canal and Hester St) Lower East Side ③
+1 212 660 0312
www.metrograph.com

Revered old films and independent new ones are on the agenda of this theater that harks back to the glam of the 1920s. Events also take the stage with exclusive premieres, rare archival print screenings, and book signings. A restaurant on the premises modeled after Hollywood backlot cafeterias, is where you'll grab a bite before/after the show.

418 NITEHAWK CINEMA

136 Metropolitan
Avenue (at Berry St)
Williamsburg ⑨
+1 718 782 8370
www.nitehawkcinema.com

If you'd like dining and cocktailing to be a part of your viewing experience, then this place is for you. Tiny tables with cup holders are stationed in between the rows of seats. Menus are sometimes themed to match the particular film – ranging from current releases to its free Simpsons Club on Monday nights.

419 SPECTACLE THEATER

124 South 3rd St
(betw Bedford Ave
and Berry St)
Williamsburg ⑨
www.spectacletheater.com

A non-profit art theater specializing in the odd, offbeat, and the extremely creative. They rescue lost films, too, which you can view for 5 dollars. Staffed entirely by volunteers immersed in the craft: filmmakers, artists, editors, and performers. The intimate space holds 27 seats, and is equipped with quality audio and projection.

420 MUSEUM OF THE MOVING IMAGE

36-01 35th Avenue
(betw 36th and 37th St)
Astoria, Queens
+1 718 777 6888
www.movingimage.us

Housed in a high tech, futuristic wonder is a theater with the biggest screen in NYC. Guest directors and actors often appear on the scene along with the films: new releases, themed festivals, and cinema classics. Ongoing and special exhibits, many interactive, are designed to thrill movie buffs.

5

TV SHOWS

with a live audience

**421 LATE SHOW WITH
STEPHEN COLBERT**
AT: ED SULLIVAN THEATER
**1697 Broadway (betw W
53rd and 54th St)
Times Square** ⑥
+1 212 975 8800
www.nytix.com

After David Letterman retired from the
Late Show comedian Stephen Colbert took
over. Tickets for the tapings go fast, and
lining up starts at 11 am for the 5.30 show.
VIP Tickets are occasionally auctioned
off (with proceeds going to charity)
and include backstage passes, priority
entrance, and access to the best seats.

**422 THE TONIGHT SHOW
STARRING
JIMMY FALLON**
AT: NBC STUDIO 6-B
COMCAST BUILDING
**30 Rockefeller Plaza
50th St entrance
Midtown** ⑥
+1 212 664 3056
www.tonightshowtix.com

Jimmy Fallon of *Saturday Night Live*'s fame
does his rendition of late night. You
should arrive no later than 3.15 pm for
the 5 pm taping if you want to be in the
audience, as they sell more tickets than
seats accommodate. Tickets are available
one month in advance online.

423 TODAY SHOW
OUTSIDE NBC STUDIO 1-A
Rockefeller Plaza
Midtown ⑥
www.visit.today.com

The *TODAY* Show airs live between 7 and 10 am – you can be part of the crowd watching through the window while waving a poster. Anchors greet the crowd at 8 am, so get there at 6 if you want to be in front. See their website for details on how to meet the hosts.

424 SATURDAY NIGHT LIVE
AT: NBC STUDIO 8-H
30 Rockefeller Plaza
Midtown ⑥
www.nytix.com

This show is famous for being a political and *zeitgeist* barometer, as well as for being the cradle for future comedy talent. You cannot choose the date for your tickets, so your best bet is to try for stand-by tickets distributed at 7 am on the morning of a taping September to May. Send an email during the month of August for the upcoming season to: snltickets@nbcunio.com

425 THE DAILY SHOW WITH TREVOR NOAH
AT: COMEDY CENTRAL
733 Eleventh Avenue
(betw W 51st and
52nd St)
+1 212 586 2477
www.showclix.com

Trevor Noah has taken the challenge of replacing Jon Stewart in this American news satire and late-night talk show, which airs Monday through Thursday on Comedy Central. Reserve up to 4 tickets online, and make sure to line up at noon to ensure entry, since reserving does not guarantee you will be admitted.

RINK AT BRYANT PARK

25 THINGS TO DO
WITH CHILDREN

The 5 best
PLAYGROUNDS

---

426 WASHINGTON SQUARE ASTROTURF PLAYGROUND

Along MacDougal St and
Washington Sq South
Greenwich Village ④
+1 212 588 5659
www.washingtonsquare
parkconservancy.org

The southwest corner of Washington Square Park contains a glossy, bright green, fake-grass area which allows kids to get a little wild. Outfitted with a rope net ladder for climbing, it sits under tall shady trees. As kids scamper about, adults can enjoy sounds of jazz from local street musicians.

427 PIER 51 PLAYGROUND

Along the West Side
Highway (at Jane St)
West Village ④
+1 212 627 2020
www.hudsonriverpark.org

This playground is situated on a pier jutting into the Hudson river and is loaded with things to climb on. Showers, sprinklers, and streams of running water allow for splashing and cooling off in the summer as does the small ice-cream and drink cart.

428 TOMPKINS SQUARE PARK

Betw Avenue A
and East 7th St
East Village ④
www.nycgovparks.org

Set squarely in the East Village and therefore, shall we say, slightly rougher around the edges, this park services the neighborhood with a traditional playground. There are grassy lawns too, next to basketball courts where older kids skateboard. A public pool straddles the northern stretch of the park.

429 **BROOKLYN BRIDGE PARK**

Along the waterfront
North and south of
Brooklyn Bridge
Brooklyn Heights ⑩
www.brooklynbridge
park.org

A welcome respite from the hustle and bustle, this green area sits right on the East River, Brooklyn side. Several piers make up this fun-filled park, outfitted with a giant slide, jungle gym, swings, carousel, and water features. Amazing views of downtown Manhattan. Kid-friendly entertainers abound during the summer.

430 **PIERREPONT PLAYGROUND**

Pierrepont Place
(end of Pierrepont St)
Brooklyn Heights ⑩
www.nycgovparks.org

Adjacent to the Brooklyn Heights Promenade with best views of the southern tip of Manhattan's Financial District. Not as flashy as other play-grounds – old school even, but the serene location gives it a homey feel. An annual Halloween parade and Easter Egg hunt are wonderful local activities kids could indulge in.

427 PIER 51 PLAYGROUND

5 of the best spots in
CENTRAL PARK
for kids

---

431 HECKSCHER PLAYGROUND

7th Avenue & Central Park South Playground runs from W 61st to 63rd St
www.centralpark.com

Oldest and largest playground in the south end of the park, with slides, swings, and seesaws and a man-made aqueduct connected to a natural rock formation. Run up the rock, go down other side to get involved in a pick-up baseball or kickball game on the Heckscher Ballfields directly to the north.

432 STATUES: HANS CHRISTIAN ANDERSON AND ALICE IN WONDERLAND

West of Conservatory Water at 74th St
www.centralpark.com

Makes for great photo ops. Anderson is depicted reading from his book *The Ugly Duckling* with duck listening attentively. Storytelling of *The Little Mermaid* and *Thumbelina* takes place during summer on Saturday mornings rain or shine. Close by is *Alice in Wonderland*, a statue kids love to climb on.

433 MODEL BOAT SAILING

Kerbs Memorial Boathouse, at E 74th St Entrance at E 72nd or 76th St
+1 917 522 0054
www.sailthepark.com

For a step back in time head to Conservatory Water. Since the late 1800s, kids have been racing model sailboats both remote controlled and wind-powered. Model sailboats can be rented. No reservations, first come first serve.

434 BALTO STATUE

West of East Drive and E 67th St, north of the Zoo.
www.centralpark.com/guide/attractions/balto.html

For dog-loving tots, take the trek to see Balto, the Siberian husky sled dog immortalized in the book and film. Just north of the Tisch Children's Zoo, Balto sits atop a rock waiting for children to climb up. A true story – his heroic deeds saved the ailing residents of Nome, Alaska.

435 CENTRAL PARK ZOO

At East 64th St and 5th Avenue
+1 212 439 6500
www.centralparkzoo.com

The east side of the park is home to an astonishing assortment of animals. Big cats gracefully jump on rocks, animated penguins and puffins enjoy a feeding, and bears explore their rocky habitat. The Tisch Children's Zoo is a special section just for kids, featuring scampering goats and potbelly pigs available for hugging and petting.

CENTRAL PARK

5 places to
ICE SKATE

**436 LEFRAK CENTER
AT LAKESIDE**

AT: PROSPECT PARK

(near the Parkside &
Ocean Ave entrance)
Brooklyn ⑪
+1 718 462 0010
www.lakesidebrooklyn.com

For ice skating in a more natural setting,
head to Brooklyn. This new 16.000-square
foot ice skating rink, opens November
through March, has an area open to the
skies, and a section under a modern
roof structure. During the summer, the
same space houses a fountain and the
Bluestone Café with indoor and outdoor
seating around.

437 THE RINK

AT: ROCKEFELLER CENTER

45 Rockefeller Plaza
(5th Ave, betw 49th
and 50th St)
Midtown ⑥
+1 212 332 7654
www.therink
atrockcenter.com

From the beginning of October thru
April, this classic ice skating rink fills
everyone with holiday cheer. Skate while
being overseen by the golden statue of
Prometheus, and other envious onlookers.
When you're done skating, delight the
kids with a visit to the best Lego store on
Fifth Ave through the Promenade.

438 **RINK**
AT: BRYANT PARK
Betw W 40th and 42nd
St and betw 5th and
6th Ave
October 30 thru
1st week of March
Midtown ⑥
+1 212 661 6640
www.bryantpark.org

Bryant Park, which sits behind the majestic New York Public Library, is slightly magical in summer but even more so in winter. Skate while listening to Frank Sinatra at this rink with a view: the green glass Verizon tower sits next to the Bank of America on 42nd Street and 6th Avenue. During the holidays, boutique shops set up kiosks.

439 **WOLLMAN RINK**
AT: CENTRAL PARK
East side of Central Park
betw E 62nd and 63rd St
Central Park ⑦
+1 212 439 6900
www.wollman
skatingrink.com

Another rink with NYC skyscrapers as the backdrop. You may remember seeing it in the climactic, but thoroughly predictable, scene at the end of the movie *Serendipity*. Open late October to early April, there's a skating school open every day that caters to parents and toddlers. Pure magic.

440 **THE RINK**
AT: BROOKFIELD PLACE WITH
GREGORY & PETUKHOV
230 Vesey St
Financial District ①
+1 917 391 8982
www.brookfieldplace
ny.com

If you want to be near the edge of the water downtown, this is the skating spot for you. Located conveniently behind the Winter Garden and near Hudson Eats and Le District food markets, this space beats Rockefeller center in terms of size. They also offer parent and child skate lessons.

5

MUSEUMS
children will love

---

441 CHILDREN'S MUSEUM OF THE ARTS

103 Charlton St
(betw Hudson and
Greenwich St)
Soho ③
+1 212 274 0986
www.cmany.org

Colorful and playful, this interactive museum for kids caters to kids ages 1 to 15 with classes that allow them to create their very own art – guided by in-house artists. Children have the space to get super creative with drawing, sculpture, sound art, and stop-motion animation. Exhibitions are designed to spark their imaginations.

442 BROOKLYN CHILDREN'S MUSEUM

145 Brooklyn Avenue
Crown Heights,
Brooklyn
+1 718 735 4400
www.brooklynkids.org

Housed under a bright yellow steel roof is a museum devoted to inspiring children. There are rooms which encourage play, while exhibits educate kids about culture and the natural world. The sensory room encourages exploration and was developed by a team of experts who welcome all, including those with autism. Artists interact with children.

443 AMERICAN MUSEUM OF NATURAL HISTORY

Central Park West
(at W 79th St)
Upper West Side ⑦
+1 212 769 5100
www.amnh.org

A behemoth of a museum – so plan ahead. Contains the Rose Center, the Hayden Planetarium, daily Space Shows and an IMAX auditorium, and the *pièce de résistance* – the titanosaur: the cast of a 122-foot-long dinosaur. Don't skip the Discovery Room on the 1st floor and the Millstein Hall of ocean life.

444 WHITNEY MUSEUM OF AMERICAN ART

99 Gansevoort St
(at Washington St)
Meatpacking District ④
+1 212 570 3600
www.whitney.org

Reasons: 1. To let your kids look at and walk thru a Renzo Piano structure. 2. Open Studio days allow kids to make art inspired by works on view. 3. Located on the High Line. 4. Comfy chairs with Hudson river views when you need a break. 5. Outdoor sculpture terraces.

445 CHILDREN'S MUSEUM OF MANHATTAN

212 West 83rd St
(betw Broadway and Amsterdam Ave)
Upper West Side ⑦
+1 212 721 1223
www.cmom.org

Immersive exhibits are the charm of this 5-story museum. Here kids up to age 6 can learn about culture, history and science in the most fun way. There are classes and workshops geared to delight children like Gross Biology – which will have kids screaming ewwwwww, and The Music in Me! taught by TV star Laurie Berkner.

5 kid-friendly
RESTO'S / BARS

446 ELLEN'S STARDUST DINER

1650 Broadway
(at W 51st St)
Times Square ⑥
+1 212 956 5151
www.ellenstardust
diner.com

Wannabee Broadway actors who wait tables to make money are here to delight your young aspiring entertainers. The singing waitstaff belt out show tunes to encourage outrageous behavior and singalongs, so you don't have to worry about your kids disrupting. See the latest YouTube video on their website and you'll get the drill.

447 HABANA OUTPOST

757 Fulton St
(at South Portland Ave)
Fort Greene, Brooklyn ⑩
+1 718 858 9500
www.habanaoutpost.com

This eco-friendly operation goes from April till October, serving the same fantastic Mexican eats as their location in Nolita. Jump on the eco-friendly bike to power the smoothie-making blender. The outdoor courtyard houses picnic benches made with recycled lumber, with a movie screen and supervised arts and crafts projects for kids.

448 SERENDIPITY 3

225 East 60th St
(betw E 2nd and 3rd Ave)
Upper East Side ⑦
+1 212 838 3531
www.serendipity3.com

An extension of the original Serendipity, made even more famous by the movie of the same name, this place boasts a menu that kids will adore. Enticing sweets like the Frrrozen hot chocolate, a sampling of sundaes and pies, along with a full menu of familiar choices include dim sum, pot pies, and meatloaf.

449 COWGIRL

519 Hudson St
(at W 10th St)
West Village ④
+1 212 633 1133
www.cowgirlnyc.com

Known as the Cowgirl Hall of Fame, this kitschy Southwestern spot debuted in the eighties wanting to attract and know neighborhood friends and families. Many a child's party has been hosted providing *piñatas* and goody bags. Get the Frito Pie, if you dare, a bastion of crunchy chips, hot chili, cheese and onions.

450 BROOKLYN FARMACY AND SODA FOUNTAIN

513 Henry St
(at Sackett St)
Carroll Gardens,
Brooklyn ⑪
+1 718 522 6260
www.brooklynfarmacy
andsodafountain.com

A soda shop where you can experience nostalgic NYC desserts: authentic sundaes topped with homemade syrups, ice-cream cones crafted in upstate NY, signature sodas, and milkshakes made to order. The vintage pharmacy setting is as Brooklyn as Brooklyn gets, attracting a hipster crowd – with kids.

THE STANDARD

25 PLACES
TO SLEEP

5 of the
HIPPEST HOTELS

---

451 11 HOWARD

11 Howard St
(at Lafayette St)
Soho ②
+1 212 235 1111
www.11howard.com

If you want to be near everything chic and unique. One of the newer hotels in town boasts eco-friendly hospitality expressed in a minimalist natural design, with major artwork throughout. Le Cou Cou and The Blond are the hotspots of the moment.

452 THE NOMAD

1170 Broadway
(at W 28th St)
Nomad ⑤
+1 212 796 1500
www.thenomadhotel.com

For those who have their fingers on the pulse. This once industrial-wholesale area is one of the latest Manhattan hoods being hip-ified. A stunning Beaux-Arts building delights, along with critically-acclaimed bar and restaurant. Guests are the only ones that can get into the Library Bar after 4 pm.

453 THE LUDLOW

180 Ludlow St (betw Stanton and Houston St)
Lower East Side ③
+1 212 432 1818
www.ludlowhotel.com

If you're looking for a cool place where New Yorkers like to hang out. Downtown and industrial style mark the scene in the lobby amidst plushy 70s leather furniture. By contrast, rooms are formally outfitted with drapes, antique beds, and sheepskin throws, with baths done in mosaic tile. Dinner at Dirty French is not to be missed.

454 THE BOWERY HOTEL

335 Bowery
(betw E 2nd and 3rd St)
East Village ④
+1 212 505 9100
www.theboweryhotel.com

For freethinkers looking to freewheel downtown. A hotel with old-world majesty expressed in faded velvet, potted palms, carved wood, layers of antique carpets and bellhops in red jackets. This is the lobby that everyone wants to get into, and makes a preference for hotel guests. Outside, the world is at your fingertips.

455 THE STANDARD

848 Washington St
(at W 13th St)
Meatpacking District ④
+1 212 645 4646
www.standardhotels.com

For those looking for stimulation. It's not just the breakfast room downstairs, the ice rink or the German beer hall – it's the action-packed location that keeps it on the edge. Steps away from the High Line, every single room has unobstructed views through floor-to-ceiling windows (which has also been known to reveal what's going on inside – wink, wink).

453 THE LUDLOW

5

MID-PRICED
and COOL hotels

456 **THE MARLTON**

5 West 8th St
(betw 5th and 6th Ave)
Greenwich Village ④
+1 212 321 0100
www.marltonhotel.com

For traditionalists looking to soak up true Greenwich Village spirit. A distinguished design has morphed this once flop house into something quite grand. Rooms are small, but beautifully appointed, with white marble baths outfitted with brass fixtures. The lobby is a popular NYC hangout. One block up from Washington Square Park.

457 **SOHO GRAND**

310 West Broadway
(betw Canal and
Grand St)
Soho ②
+1 212 965 3000
www.sohogrand.com

For those who plan on hitting all the designer shops. Still trendy, who can resist the comfortable, voluptuous lounges which grace the second floor. You can totally relax in the comfy upscale rooms too, decked out in beiges and taupes, knowing that you are near to all that is Soho, but at the quieter end of the spectrum.

458 ARCHER HOTEL

45 West 38th St
(betw 5th and 6th Ave)
Midtown ⑥
+1 212 719 4100
www.archerhotel.com

If you're looking for views for less cash.
A sprawling 22-story hotel in an area that's close to everything, but a little off the beaten track. Celebrity chef David Burke's Fabrick restaurant is a treat to have off the lobby, and the rooftop bar Spyglass has winning views of the Empire State Building. Rooms are small but smartly laid out, with thoughtful touches.

459 GILD HALL

15 Gold St (betw Platt St
and Maiden Lane)
Financial District ①
+1 212 232 7700
www.thompsonhotels.com

If you want to stay in the oldest part of Manhattan. Don't let the plain brick facade fool you. Inside is a jewel of a hotel sporting the tone of a gentleman's lodge – in tanned leather and polished wood. Rooms are sizable with marble baths. Close to subways for when you want to whisk uptown.

460 WALKER HOTEL

52 West 13th St
(betw 5th and 6th Ave)
Greenwich Village ④
+1 212 375 1300
www.walkerhotel.com

If you love the village and walking everywhere. Gas lanterns adorn the entryway in this hotel evoking past times. The lobby is somewhat grand with velvet couches and a fireplace, and rooms are decently sized and priced, with Art-Deco flavor. Lots to do in any direction from the front door.

5
HIGH-END
hotels

461 **THE MARK**
25 East 77th St
(at Madison Ave)
Upper East Side ⑦
+1 212 744 4300
www.themarkhotel.com

For the high-minded design connoisseur.
A hotel with an edgy, posh design by
Jacques Grange situated in Manhattan's
most elegant neighborhood. Providing
care and services beyond the 5-star
standard, private local phone numbers
can be assigned, or a car with driver, and
lucky kids can be treated to indoor tents
and cookies from The Mark, Jean-Georges
Vongerichten's restaurant.

462 **THE PIERRE**
2 East 61st St
(at 5th Ave)
Upper East Side ⑦
+1 212 838 8000
www.thepierreny.com

If you're looking for timeless, old-world luxury.
Featured in many films, history and
beauty is what you'll find here. See the
newly restored murals in The Rotunda
(find Jackie O.). Off the lobby is the Two
E Bar, one of the classiest, undiscovered
rooms in NYC great to meet up for a
cocktail, snack, or afternoon tea. Rooms
are sedately decked out.

463 NOMO

9 Crosby St
(betw Howard and
Grand St)
Soho ②
+1 646 218 6400
www.nomosoho.com

If you love a fantasy and shopping.
Inspired by Jean Cocteau's *La Belle et la Bête*, this hotel lures you in through a dramatic courtyard of ivy-clad, metal framework. Its glass-roof restaurant is highlighted by sunlight flooding its groupings of chandeliers. Special services include personalized shopping experiences and in-room custom suit design.

464 WILLIAM VALE HOTEL

111 North 12th St
(betw Wythe Ave
and Berry St)
Williamsburg ⑨
+1 718 631 8400
www.thewilliamvale.com

If you want to do Williamsburg in style.
A spectacular, futuristic design by Albo Liberis perches dramatically above Brooklyn. Every single room features work of local artists, and has a balcony with unobstructed views. The rooftop bar is the new hot spot, capitalizing on its height with viewing scopes stationed around the space for an even closer look.

465 CROSBY STREET HOTEL

79 Crosby St
(betw Prince and
Spring St)
Soho ②
+1 212 226 6400
www.firmdalehotels.com

If you are looking for homey elegance.
The scale and peacefulness of this eco-conscious hotel is immediately felt upon entering. Newly built, each room is uniquely styled by London designer Kit Kemp and has industrial oversized windows to bring in the light. Crosby Bar is a popular NY meeting spot for cocktails and afternoon tea.

5 hotels for a
SHOESTRING BUDGET

466 POD 39 HOTEL

145 East 39th St
(betw 3rd and
Lexington Ave)
Murray Hill ⑥
+1 212 865 5700
www.thepodhotel.com

For those whose only desire is to be out and about. Streamlined, compact rooms offer just what you need to stay in NYC and have extra cash to run around with. Whimsical rooftop space, hot-spot Salvation Taco, and a colorful lobby with room to relax or play a game of ping-pong can be your temporary havens.

467 THE GATSBY HOTEL

135 E Houston St
(at Forsythe St)
Lower East Side ③
+1 212 358 8844
www.gatsbyhotelnyc.com

If you are looking to hit all the bars on the Lower East Side. An unassuming brick building with simple and tastefully sparse rooms sits on the border of the LES, East Village, and Nolita neighborhoods. Staff is friendly and accommodating. Note: some rooms are in the basement (C level).

468 THE JANE HOTEL

113 Jane St
(betw Washington
and West St)
Meatpacking District ④
+1 212 924 6700
www.thejanenyc.com

If you're just looking for a room to crash in a happening hotel. Teeny tiny rooms, most without a private bath, with Victorian styling, that once housed survivors from the Titanic. The good news is that you'll be IN at the grandiose, lively bar downstairs, and are situated in a most fantastic part of town.

469 COLONIAL HOUSE INN

318 West 22nd St
(betw 8th and 9th Ave)
Chelsea ⑤
+1 212 243 9669
www.colonialhouseinn.com

For those who prefer an intimate setting.
A bed-and-breakfast with a decidedly
gay clientele, but open to all. Half the
20 rooms have private baths. Suites are
available and sleep up to 5 guests, one
facing a private garden and the other
with kitchenette. Founded by Mel Cheren,
known as 'The Godfather of Disco'.

470 RIFF CHELSEA HOTEL

300 West 30th St
(at 8th Ave)
Chelsea ⑤
+1 212 244 7827
www.riffchelsea.com

If you're looking for just the basics. Located in
no-man's-land near Chelsea and Nomad,
you'll find a cheerful hotel with compact,
optically-graphic rooms and an 80s rock
theme. You'll have to share a bath in
some rooms, there's a suite perfect for
those with kids, or a group suite that
sleeps up to 12. Outdoor courtyard.
No elevators.

468 THE JANE HOTEL

5 boutique hotels
OUTSIDE MANHATTAN

---

471 MCCARREN HOTEL AND POOL

160 North 12th St
(betw Bedford Ave
and Berry St)
Williamsburg ⑨
+1 718 218 7500
www.mccarrenhotel.com

For those with bathing suit bods. This hotel's rooms look down upon one of New York's largest swimming pools. It carries a minimalist, yet happy design, with pops of color throughout, especially in Sheltering Sky, its rooftop bar providing views and craft cocktails. Oleanders serves brunch on the weekends from 10 to 3 pm.

472 THE BROOKLYN — A HOTEL

199 Atlantic Avenue
(betw Clinton and
Court St)
Brooklyn Heights,
Brooklyn ⑩
+1 718 789 1500
www.thebrooklynny.com

If you're planning on exploring Brooklyn for less. Located in the rapidly-gentrifying, though still gritty, Bed-Stuy neighborhood, about a half hour subway ride from Manhattan. Guestrooms are spacious, laid out railroad style with one room leading to the next, with nostalgic murals of Brooklyn architectural icons. Slick bathrooms. No room service, but breakfast buffet in the lobby.

473 BORO HOTEL

38-28 27th St (betw
38th and 39th Ave)
Long Island City
+1 718 433 1375
www.borohotel.com

If you want to be near the ethnic eats of Astoria. Across from the Upper East Side of Manhattan is yet another area getting a modern makeover. This new hotel's got the views – plus the nice price. Rooms feature a wall of windows, balconies, against a backdrop of raw cinderblocks and white oak floors. Rooftop, of course.

474 THE WILLIAMSBURG HOTEL

96 Wythe Avenue
(at N 10th St)
Williamsburg ⑨
+1 718 362 8100
www.thewilliamsburg
hotel.com

For those on the cutting edge. An austere slim exterior belies the stylish delights within. Beckoning, rich-turquoise tiled baths with brass fixtures, a mix of tufted natural leather and cool reclaimed wood parquet floors add to the homey digs. Three separate bars, including one on the roof disguised as a water tower.

475 NU HOTEL

85 Smith St
(betw Atlantic Ave
and State St)
Brooklyn Heights,
Brooklyn ⑩
+1 718 852 8585
www.nuhotelbrooklyn.com

For the movers and shakers. Experience clean lines with touches of glamour, in one of downtown Brooklyn's original boutique hotels. Playful touches like hammocks and colorful murals painted by street artists make each room interesting. Stay fit at the 24/7 fitness center or borrow one of their cool designer bikes.

CONEY ISLAND

25 ACTIVITIES FOR WEEKENDS

The 5 best
DAY TRIP
destinations

---

476 SANDY HOOK BEACH FERRY

3 Locations in
Manhattan
+1 800 262 8743
*seastreak.com/daytrips-
and-getaways/sandy-hook-
beach/*

Enjoy a cocktail on the roof as you speed through the harbor, then shuttle to the beach – in 40 minutes flat. There's a family-friendly beach, as well as a clothing-optional stretch at the end, where gay men go to flaunt. Bring your own lunch, or cash for the food trucks. Leave early, beaches fill up quickly.

477 ASBURY PARK

Ocean Avenue
(betw Asbury and
Sunset Ave)
Asbury Park, NJ
+1 732 897 6500
www.apboardwalk.com

Check out the beachy getaway that's getting upgraded in cool. Off the boardwalk are the hipster-y Asbury Hotel and über-German Asbury *Festhalle & Biergarten*. Talula's is for healthy pizza. Storehouse is where you shop for local designers wares. 1,5 hours by car or 2 hours by train from NYC.

478 DIA: BEACON

3 Beekman St
Beacon, NY
+1 845 440 0100
www.diaart.org

Near the train station is a museum housing art on a massive scale. Spaces are dedicated to major conceptual artists of the 60s. Oversized rooms act as part of the viewing experience. After, head to Beacon Flea Market for handcrafted merch, and Denning's Point Distillery for tastings and music.

479 NORTH FORK WINE TOURS

714 Main St.
Greenport, NY
Long Island
+1 631 723 0505
*www.northfork
winetours.com*

Enjoy the quieter tip of Long Island – over 40 wineries sit amongst the vineyards for a pastoral escape. Packages include round trip transportation, tastings at 3 vineyards/breweries. A picnic lunch is available, or dine at a winery while listening to live music and learning first-hand what Long Island wines are all about.

480 GOVERNORS ISLAND

New York Harbor
www.govisland.com

From May to October, an island right in Manhattan's harbor can feel a million miles away. A perfect spot for a picnic, bike ride, or just strolling around and admiring the view. They also host events, like their annual art fairs, storytelling and poetry festivals, so check the calendar. Ferries leave from Manhattan and Brooklyn.

477 ASBURY PARK

The 5 cosiest ways
to spend a weekend in the
CATSKILLS

---

481 HIKING

www.catskillmountaineer.
com/hiking.html

Your guide for maneuvering through the wilderness – on foot. This site gives you topographical maps of hiking areas throughout the Catskills, marking out mileage and trek times, difficulty ratings, and descriptions of terrain. Structures are highlighted, and are paired with photos of the trails. GPS coordinates get you started. Now all you need is a nice picnic lunch.

482 SPRUCETON INN

2080 Spruceton Road
West Kill, NY
+1 518 989 6404
www.sprucetoninn.com

You can almost smell the crisp air viewing the photos on the website. Tucked in the hills of West Kill, is this B&B – standing for Bed and Bar – with super sparse, rustic rooms. Grounds offer fire pits, and no light pollution, so night skies are filled with stars. Kitchenettes and BBQs allow you to whip up something from local farms.

482 SPRUCETON INN

481 HIKING

251

483 WEST KILL BREWING

2191 Spruceton Road
West Kill, NY
+1 518 989 6462
www.westkillbrewing.com

In the middle of pristine nowhere, you'll find beer made with locally grown and foraged ingredients the same way early settlers in the area did. Sample fruity beers made with sour cherries, elderberries, lingonberries and apples – or some uncommon flavors from local mushrooms and spruce tips. This 127-acre family farm is situated along the road with the best hiking trails.

484 BRUSHLAND EATING HOUSE

1927 County Highway 6
Bovina Center, NY
+1 607 832 4861
www.brushland
eatinghouse.com

An inn, restaurant, and shop modeling itself on colonial times when 'eating houses' were the only socializing hub. On this single street town, the restaurant offers a simple, elegant menu run by a trio of Brooklyn ex-pats. Try one of their seasonal toasts. Stay in one of their airy rooms filled with rustic wooden furniture and accessories.

485 THE BEAR CAFÉ

295 Tinker St (Route 212)
Woodstock, NY
+1 845 679 5555
www.bearcafe.com

In a former haunt of rock and roll bands, childhood friends reunited to create an upscale dining experience perched idyllically on a stream. A four-sided bar dominates the space clad in wood-paneling with hand-hewn wooden beams and a lovely fireplace. The restaurant sits next to the Bearsville Theater, where you can still hear big acts and local bands play.

5 scenic places for
ANTIQUEING+

486 LAMBERTVILLE HOUSE

32 Bridge St
Lambertville, NJ
+1 609 397 0200
www.lambertville
house.com

Historically enchanting, Lambertville was founded in 1705 and retains much of the architecture from its past. Great for shopping – they're known for their antique stores – strolling along the river, and enjoying their foodie nooks, like Lambertville House, also a hotel. For kids, the Howell Living History Farm lets them see what farm life was like in the early 1900s. New Hope, a town across the river, is more commercial.

487 VILLAGE OF COLD SPRING

85 Main St
Cold Spring, NY
+1 845 265 3611
www.coldspringny.gov

Take the train up the scenic Hudson Line to a charming river town. Main Street heads up from the station and is lined on both sides with affordable vintage shops, galleries, and restaurants. Hike up Little Stony Point for views of the river or through the trails at West Point Foundry Preserve, an outdoor museum.

488 THE TIME NYACK

400 High Avenue
Nyack, NY
+1 845 675 8700
www.thetimehotels.com/
nyack

Along the Hudson, NJ side, is a quaint town known for its shopping and restaurants. The Time, its new boutique hotel, is perched at the top of town. Hike in Hook Mountain. Across the Hudson, explore Kykuit, a Rockefeller estate, the Lyndhurst Mansion, and dine at famous Blue Hill at Stone Barns restaurant.

489 HYDE PARK MANSION HOPPING

4097 Albany Post Road
Hyde Park, NY
+1 845 229 9115
www.nps.gov/vama

Compare and contrast two mansions in a day! Vanderbilt's, and the home of Franklin Delano Roosevelt. In town, cool Main Street awaits, and a quick drive brings you to the revered Culinary Institute of America. B&B's are scattered about as well as some decent inexpensive chain hotels. Nearby Poughkeepsie offers the scenic walkway over the Hudson.

490 TOUR OF HUDSON NEW YORK

www.gotohudson.net

A 2,5-hour drive brings you to Hudson, a town of historic buildings, antique stores, and the spot where Manhattan VIPs have weekend houses. We love: 26 Warren B&B and Rivertown Lodge, The Spotty Dog Books & Ale, Ca'Mea, Moto Coffee Machine. For art: Olana State Historic Site. You can also get there via Amtrak.

5 great escapes in the
OTHER BOROUGHS

---

491 **WAVE HILL**

West 249th St
(at Independence Ave)
Riverdale, The Bronx
+1 718 549 3200
www.wavehill.org

Situated high above the Hudson is a 28-acre park whose panoramas have not changed since 1843. Stroll through its many gardens and greenhouse. A mansion on the grounds features art exhibits and a cafe. Download self-guided tours. Take the train from Grand Central to Riverdale, or the 1 subway line to the end – then free Wave Hill shuttle.

492 **CITY ISLAND**

on the Long Island
Sound
The Bronx
www.cityisland.com

A quaint island lined with Victorian homes, Italian restaurants specializing in fresh seafood, and a marina. Jack's Bait & Tackle offers 4-person fiberglass boats, The New York Sailing Center has sailing classes. Less than 1,5 hour away. 6 train to Pelham Bay Park. Transfer to the BX 29 bus towards City Island.

495 CONEY ISLAND

493 FOODIE TOUR: ASTORIA

30th Avenue and
Ditmars Boulevard
Astoria, Queens

Queens is the most diverse of all the boroughs in NYC, and its eateries span the globe. Start out on Ditmars Blvd (The Pomeroy), serpentine from 30th to 33rd Ave: Il Bambino (great panini), Milkflower, Vesta, Queens Comfort, Sugar Freak. For Greek food: Taverna Kyclades, Astoria Seafood, Bahari Estiatoro, Agnanti. South on Steinway is Little Egypt with hookah lounges and Mombar.

494 FORAGE TOURS

+1 914 835 2153
www.wildman
stevebrill.com

Local character Steve Brill leads nature walks which teach you to identify edible plants. Learn to distinguish something edible from something deadly in The Bronx, Brooklyn, Queens, Westchester, and Putnam counties. Steve Brill leads tours on a regular basis, with a suggested donation of 20 dollars. Check the extensive schedule and sign up for an interesting experience.

495 CONEY ISLAND

Corbin Place
to West 37 St
Coney Island,
Brooklyn
+1 718 946 1353
www.coneyisland.com

Coney Island offers its kitschy attractions, plus beach volleyball, a playground and an amusement park with history – and the beach, where basically anything goes. Hit Nathan's hot dog emporium. Take a spin on the antique roller coasters and ferris wheel. Witness daily feedings at the NY Aquarium. See the schedule of summer concerts and the famous Mermaid Parade.

5

LONG ISLAND

treasures

---

496 POLLOCK-KRASNER HOUSE AND STUDY CENTER

830 Springs-Fireplace Road
East Hampton, NY
+1 631 324 4929
www.stonybrook.edu/pkhouse

Tour the house where artists Jackson Pollock and his wife Lee Krasner drank, fought, and made art. Original floorboards with paint of Pollock's most famous poured paintings can be viewed, along with the couple's furnishings, as well as exhibits with a special focus on local artists' work. Open from May to October. Check the calendar for who's speaking at the lecture series.

497 OCEAN BEACH

Fire Island
+1 631 687 4750
nps.gov/fiis

On this car-free island, composed of private homes and natural parks, is Ocean Beach – one of the few areas with restaurants, bars, and boutiques along the sandy shore. Nighttime is for dancing and partying. No food or drinks allowed on the beach, though. Taste of Fire Island – discounted dinner specials – happen midweek. LIRR from Penn station, then a ferry, 2,5 hours.

498 SAGG MAIN BEACH

315 Sagg Main St
Sagaponack, NY
+1 631 728 8585

This is one of those off-the-beaten-path, local beaches – if that's possible in the Hamptons – where the share-house occupants go for sun and fun. Open to the public, but you'll need a parking permit – a 25-dollar daily pass is required for non-residents, plus one for 4x4 access. Parking is ample. Catch the super-chill drum circles which gather on Monday nights and dance on the sand.

499 TOPPING ROSE HOUSE

One Bridgehampton/
Sag Harbor Turnpike
Bridgehampton, NY
+1 631 537 0870
www.toppingrose
house.com

This 1000+-dollar hotel has winter pricing at 295 dollars a night. The most charming 1842 Greek Revival mansion has a hidden spa and sleek modern design. Loaner bikes available, as well as loaner Lexuses, plus shuttle rides and free passes to the beach. There's also a farm-to-table restaurant helmed by a chef you may have heard of: Jean-Georges Vongerichten.

500 SHELTER ISLAND

Mashomack Preserve
Long Island, NY
+1 631 749 1001
www.shelter-island.org

Acquired by The Nature Conservancy in the 1980s, roughly one-third of Shelter Island is dedicated to protecting rare plant species and birds – especially breeding ospreys. To maintain the habitat, they strictly enforce a 'no pets or food' as you hike through the winding pathways. Book a tour. Get there via Uber/Lyft from the North Haven/South Ferry.

INDEX

COLOPHON

EDITING AND COMPOSING — Michiel Vos and Ellen Swandiak

GRAPHIC DESIGN — Joke Gossé and Tinne Luyten

PHOTOGRAPHY — Erinn Springer – www.springerinn.com

ADDITIONAL PHOTOGRAPHY — Aliza Fox – p. 251: Casey Scieszka

PHOTOGRAPHY PRODUCTION — Anneliese Kristedja

COVER IMAGE — La Plaza Cultural Community Garden,
648 East 9th St, East Village (secret 501)

The addresses in this book have been selected after thorough independent research
by the authors, in collaboration with Luster Publishers. The selection is solely based
on personal evaluation of the business by the authors. Nothing in this book was
published in exchange for payment or benefits of any kind.

D/2017/12.005/6
ISBN 978 94 6058 1779
NUR 506

© 2017, Luster, Antwerp
Second edition, March 2018 — Second reprint, March 2018
www.lusterweb.com — www.the500hiddensecrets.com
info@lusterweb.com

Printed in Italy by Printer Trento.

MIX
Paper from
responsible sources
FSC® C015829